UNIVERSITY OF OXFORD
PITT RIVERS MUSEUM

Monograph Series No. 1

ESKIMOS
OF
NORTHWEST ALASKA
IN THE
EARLY NINETEENTH CENTURY

Based on the Beechey and Belcher Collections
and records compiled during the voyage
of H. M. S. Blossom to Northwest Alaska
in 1826 and 1827

BY

J. R. BOCKSTOCE

B. LITT., D. PHIL. (Oxon)

Edited by T. K. PENNIMAN

1977

DESIGNED AND PRODUCED BY
OXPRINT LIMITED OXFORD

ESKIMOS
OF
NORTHWEST ALASKA
IN THE
EARLY NINETEENTH CENTURY

COVER PICTURE
Drawing of a woman and child
made by Captain F. W. Beechey
at Icy Cape.

EDITORS' PREFACE

We are happy to be able to publish two of our older ethnographic collections, this time those made by Captain Frederick Beechey and Lieutenant Edward Belcher during the voyage of H.M.S. *Blossom*, from the Eskimos of Northwestern Alaska before they had much contact with Europeans.

Dr. John Bockstoce, the Curator of Ethnology at the Old Dartmouth Historical Society Whaling Museum in New Bedford, Massachusetts, has added to a detailed catalogue of 119 items, an account of the collectors, their crew, observations of native behaviour and charts of their surveys of the regions visited, a good number of extracts from their journals, and several of their sketches, all of which add considerably to the value of the book.

Dr. Bockstoce has thanked the Staff of the Museum in his introduction. The Editors would like to reinforce his thanks, and to pay special tribute to Mrs. Elizabeth Sandford Gunn for her prolonged and valuable work on the manuscript.

T. K. P.
B. M. B.

Pitt Rivers Museum
Department of Ethnology
*   and Prehistory*
University of Oxford.

TO LAURIE KINGIK

TABLE OF CONTENTS

LIST OF ILLUSTRATIONS

LIST OF MAPS

ACKNOWLEDGEMENTS

Many people helped in the preparation of this catalogue, and I am grateful for their generous assistance. Mr. Bernard Fagg, Curator of the Pitt Rivers Museum, his successor Mr. Bryan Cranstone, and Mr. Ray Inskeep (Acting Curator during the interregnum) were encouraging in the preparation of the catalogue. The gathering of the collections from many areas was efficiently done by Mr. Kenneth Walters and Mr. Robert Rivers, often in difficult circumstances. The photography was carried out excellently—as always—by Mr. Peter Narracott and Mr. Rory Murphy. Mr. John Todd kindly made the line drawings of the rain shirts, Miss Beatrice Blackwood was of much help with her vast knowledge of the Pitt Rivers Museum's collections and I am indebted to Mrs. Elizabeth Sandford Gunn for unstintingly giving so much of her time to all phases of the artefact analysis and manuscript preparation.

Dr. Alan Cooke of the Scott Polar Research Institute, University of Cambridge, was helpful in locating manuscript sources and suggesting changes in the text. Other people who freely gave me information and allowed me the use of their manuscripts and collections are Mr. Basil Stuart-Stubbs, University of British Columbia; Dr. Barry Gough, Wilfred Laurier University; Mr. Archibald Hanna and Miss Joan Hoffman, Beinecke Rare Book and Manuscript Library, Yale University; Dr. W. Gillies Ross, Bishops University; Dr. Ernest S. Burch, Jr. University of Manitoba; Lieutenant Commander Andrew David, R.N. (ret.), Miss W. J. Perry and Mr. David Langmead, Hydrographic Department, Ministry of Defence (N), Taunton, Somerset; Mr. Rod Kidman and Miss Penny Bateman, The British Museum (Ethnography); Mrs. Ethel Herron, Holywood, County Down; Mr. Elmer Rasmuson, Anchorage, Alaska; Sir Giles Loder, Bart.; and the staff of the library and map rooms of the Royal Geographical Society.

Special thanks are due to Dorothy Jean Ray who generously offered her comments on early Arctic voyages and drill bows, to Marjorie S. Tomas and Mr. T. K. Penniman for their editorial assistance, and to Miss Ann Hechle for drawing the maps. The Rt. Hon. The Earl of Verulam gave special assistance throughout the undertaking. Mr. Nigel Blackwell was most helpful with the publication of the text.

Logistical support at Point Barrow, Alaska, was provided by the U.S. Naval Arctic Research Laboratory.

I am indebted to Mr. Laurie Kingik of Point Hope, Alaska—to whom this catalogue is dedicated—for stimulating my interest in Eskimo material culture and for kindly and patiently teaching me about it.

J. R. B.
Gorhambury
St. Albans
Herts.

April, 1975

INTRODUCTION

INTRODUCTION

Captain Frederick William Beechey and Lieutenant Edward Belcher made significant collections of Eskimo artefacts in northwestern Alaska during the voyage of H.M.S. *Blossom* in 1826 and 1827 and many of these artefacts are now in the collections of the Pitt Rivers Museum at Oxford University. The Beechey and Belcher collections are important to anthropologists and historians because they are the first large collections made in northwestern Alaska.

Before presenting a description and analysis of the artefacts in the Beechey and Belcher collections, it will be useful to place the voyage of the *Blossom* in historical perspective. A review of contacts made by Asians and Europeans with the inhabitants of the Bering Strait region prior to 1826 will be followed by a discussion of the events leading up to the *Blossom*'s voyage.

Exploration and Contact in the Bering Strait Region

Two Cossacks, Semen Dezhnev and Fedot Alexeev, were probably the first people with a western culture to pass through Bering Strait. They came—nine years after the first Russians had reached the Pacific Ocean—in 1648 (Lebedev and Grekov, 1967:170).

Ray (n.d. *a*) believes that "Dezhnev's report contained the first ethnographic information about Little Diomede Island people, who belonged culturally, and later politically, to western Alaska. He said that men of the 'Islands' wore pieces of bone in their chins. These ornaments, or labrets, were not used by Siberians. The ambiguous language of the report suggests that this news could have been learned without going to Bering Strait, because Alaskan Eskimos were sometimes prisoners of the Chukchef, and Dezhnev would have had the opportunity to see or hear about them in northeastern Siberia".

Indirect contact between Alaskan Eskimos and people of other cultures had been established nearly fifteen hundred years earlier, however, through the trade in iron, which passed into Alaska from Asia (Larsen and Rainey, 1948:82-83; Larsen, 1951:83-88). Indirect trade contacts must have increased considerably soon after Dezhnev and Alexeev's voyage, for in 1649 Dezhnev built a fort on the Anadyr River in Siberia (Armstrong, 1965:24) and by about 1675 several trading posts had been established near the Chukotsk Peninsula (Map 1) (Golder, 1914:28-29).

In 1728 Vitus Bering, a Dane serving in the Russian Navy, commanded the second expedition to pass north of Bering Strait. He reached 67°18'48" north latitude at about 168° west longitude (Lebedev and Grekov, 1967:175), but poor visibility kept him from seeing the American shore when he passed through the strait (Golder, 1914:142-45). Four years later Fedorov and Gvozdev sailed to Bering Strait from Kamchatka. They landed on one of the Diomede Islands and approached the coast of Alaska to the south of Cape Prince of Wales, where they met a native of King Island in a boat (Lebedev and Grekov, 1967:178). One product of their voyage was the charting of the shores of Bering Strait (Jefferys, 1761). Following that expedition, Ivan Sindt, having sailed from Okhotsk in 1764, reached the southwest corner of the Seward Peninsula, probably near Cape Rodney, in 1767 (Coxe, 1780:300-302).

The pioneering voyages of the Russians are of great historical importance, but early Russian contributions to geographical knowledge were overshadowed by the explorations of Captain James Cook. Cook reached Arctic waters in his third voyage from England, in 1778, while

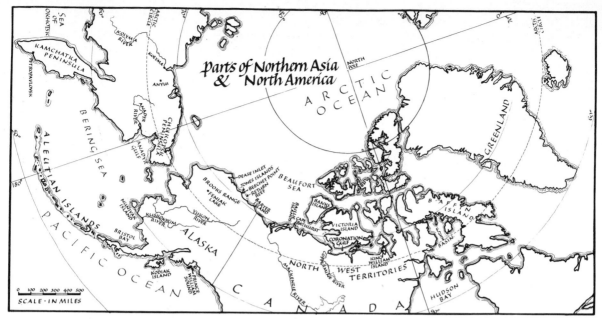

Map 1. Parts of Northeastern Asia and North America

seeking a northwest passage connecting the Atlantic and Pacific oceans. He accurately surveyed in the Bering Strait region and along the coast of northwestern Alaska. On the American shore he reached lat. 70°41′ N. before being stopped by ice, and he named his farthest point Icy Cape (Map 2). He then surveyed part of the northern coast of the Chukotsk Peninsula and Norton Sound. The following winter he was killed in the Hawaiian Islands, and the leadership of the expedition passed to Charles Clerke. Clerke passed through Bering Strait in 1779 and was also stopped by heavy pack ice. Although Cook and Clerke mapped the coast of much of northwestern Alaska, they failed to discover two important bodies of water, Kotzebue Sound and Port Clarence. Neither man conducted a coastal survey in the latitude of Kotzebue Sound

Map 2. Part of Northwestern Alaska

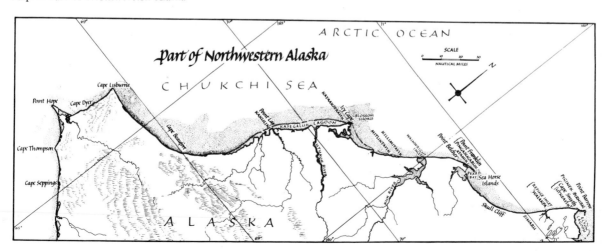

(Map 3), and they did not discover Port Clarence because a low sand spit, Point Spencer, forms an embayment that makes the body of water beyond difficult to see from a distance.

Cook's last voyage apparently stimulated further Russian interest in northern Alaska both for political and for commercial reasons. In fact, Cook sent his reports overland to England, and it is possible that the Russians knew of his discoveries before the British did (Foote, 1965:26). It is also possible that this knowledge contributed to the despatch of Ivan Kobelev's expedition overland to Bering Strait in 1779. Kobelev was able to reach only Little Diomede Island (Masterson and Brower, 1948:93-94: Ray, 1971:4); but when the results of his voyage were published in 1784, it is likely that other nations were prompted to undertake explorations in the area. A French expedition under La Perouse was sent to the northwest coast of North America in 1785, and at the same time the Empress of Russia ordered a secret expedition organized under the leadership of Joseph Billings, an Englishman, and Gavrul Sarychev, a Russian (Baker, 1906:61-62). Billings had been an astronomer's assistant on Cook's third voyage. He was despatched by the Russian Crown to explore in the Bering Strait region, among other objectives. After a short, abortive trip from the south of the Kolyma River in 1787, he sailed from Kamchatka in the *Glory of Russia* in 1791. Landing at Cape Rodney, he met natives there and then sailed to St. Lawrence Bay on the Chukotsk Peninsula, where he ordered his ship back to Kamchatka.

Ivan Kobelev also took part in that expedition. In 1791 he returned to Bering Strait and

Map 3. The Bering Strait Region

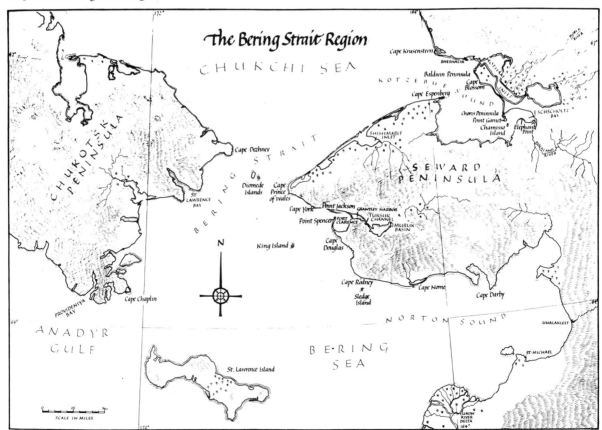

reached King Island and the mouth of Port Clarence in umiaks (Fedorova, 1973:4) before Billings reached the area. Billings then continued exploring the coast of northeastern Siberia by native skin boat, finishing his journey by land in 1792 (Sauer, 1802). After his return, no expeditions are known to have entered the Bering Strait region until about 1816.

After the end of the Napoleonic wars both Great Britain and Russia showed a renewed interest in the Bering Strait region as an entrance to a northwest passage. The first of the expeditions sent there was from Russia, and it was led by Otto von Kotzebue, a German who left Kronstadt in 1815 and arrived in the Bering Strait region a year later. He first visited the natives of St. Lawrence Island and then passed through Bering Strait, anchoring at Shishmaref Inlet, which he named for his assistant, Capt. Lt. G. S. Shishmarev (Orth, 1971:867). Sailing on, he passed into Kotzebue Sound (Map 4), which Cook had not surveyed, and met Eskimos there (Choris, 1822, Plate 1) (Plate 1). He anchored near Choris Peninsula and Chamisso Island (Map 5), naming them for his ship's artist, Louis Choris, and naturalist, Louis Adelbert von Chamisso (Orth, 1971:198, 215). Next he explored Eschscholtz Bay and named it after the ship's physician, Dr. Frederick Eschscholtz (Orth, 1971:317; von Kotzebue, 1821:I, 189-240).

Map 4. Beechey's Chart of Kotzebue Sound

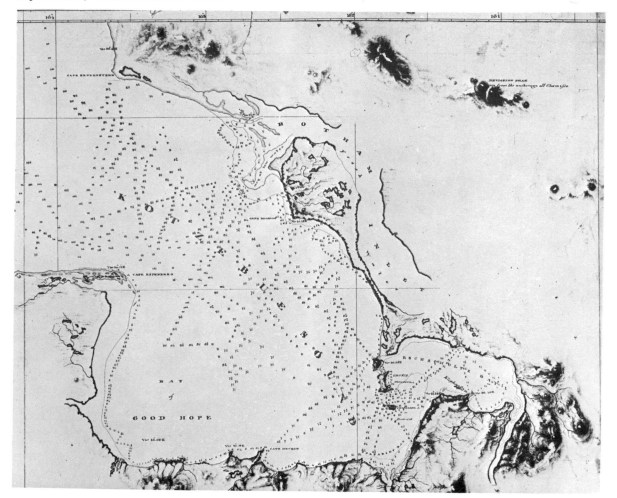

Von Kotzebue sailed south in August, 1816, and returned the next year, but only reached St. Lawrence Island.

Von Kotzebue's claim to have independently discovered the sound that bears his name is questionable (Foote, 1965:34-39). It seems likely that information about the sound, perhaps derived from natives of the Bering Strait region, had been passed to Europeans well before the date of von Kotzebue's voyage. John Cochrane, an Englishman visiting Kamchatka, commented that the Russians had been aware of Kotzebue Sound for "more than one hundred years" (Cochrane, 1824:262). As Foote points out (1965:34-39), it is possible that the wide geographic knowledge possessed by most natives in the Bering Strait region was passed, via the Chukchees, to foreign explorers.

Before von Kotzebue's voyage the Russian-American Company, a fur trading company chartered by the Czar to operate in Alaska, had restricted its trading activities to southern Alaska, but in the second decade of the nineteenth century it began to take an active interest in the northern regions. To some extent the renewed Russian interest was probably a response to increasing British fur-trading activity in northwestern Canada and to the territorial claims accompanying such activity. This may have been the reason why an American, Captain Gray, possibly sailing John Jacob Astor's brig *Sylph*, was sent north by the Russians to check the accuracy of von Kotzebue's surveys. Whether Gray carried out the Russians' orders is a matter

Map 5. Beechey's Chart of the Chamisso Island Anchorage

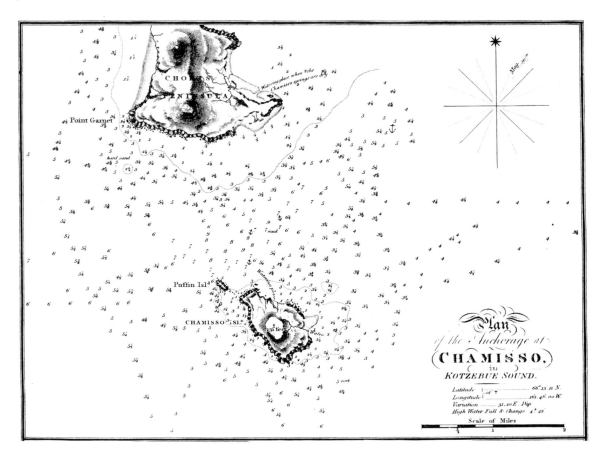

of dispute, but in 1819 he passed through Bering Strait, anchored his brig off Shishmaref Inlet, and from there continued by small boat along the north shore of Seward Peninsula. During this voyage he traded firearms and ammunition, probably for Eskimo furs and ivory (Foote, 1965:45-54; Ray, 1975).

In 1819 another expedition, composed of two ships under the command of M. N. Vasiliev and G. S. Shishmarev, von Kotzebue's former lieutenant, was sent from Kronstadt toward Bering Strait to seek a passage to the Atlantic Ocean. This expedition did not have the commercial intent of Gray's voyage. The ships arrived in Kotzebue Sound in 1820 and probably carried out surveys of the coast between Cape Krusenstern and Icy Cape. One of the ships reached lat. 71°06' N. and, in the process, discovered Point Hope peninsula where two settlements, comprising about six hundred people, were located. In 1821 the ships returned to the north of Bering Strait and reached Icy Cape again before being stopped by ice (Foote, 1965:57-58; Lebedev and Grekov, 1967:197; VanStone, 1973:11-19).

At Elephant Point in July of the previous year, 1820, a party from one of the Russian ships encountered about three hundred Eskimos from the Buckland River who were camped in tents. They noticed that some of the natives had firearms, and later, when hostilities broke out between the Russians and Eskimos, the two groups exchanged gunfire. The second Russian ship sailed into Kotzebue Sound at about this time, followed by another of Astor's brigs, the *Pedler* under the command of Captain William Pigot who announced his intention of trading firearms and ammunition with the Eskimos in return for furs. In addition to the *Pedler* and *Sylph*, four other United States vessels may have been operating in the waters near Bering Strait between 1815 and 1820 (Howay, 1973:141-42; Ray, 1975).

As a result of the increasing presence of United States trading ships in Alaska, the Russian-American Company, desirous of maintaining its trade monopoly but lacking the power to enforce it, inaugurated a policy of secrecy. This may have come about also because of England's increasing activities in western Canada and the British attempt in 1818 to find a northwest passage from the Atlantic Ocean. Because of Russian secrecy it is impossible to determine what other Russian explorations may have taken place in the Bering Strait region and northern Alaska (Foote, 1965:59-61).

We do know, though, that the Russian-American Company sponsored another Russian exploratory expedition in 1821. V. S. Khromchenko and A. K. Etolin were in command of the two ships of the expedition, and from 1821 to 1822 they carried out coastal surveys, primarily in the Norton Sound area, although they did pass north of Bering Strait (VanStone, 1973). At this same time, from 1820 to 1824, a land expedition under Ferdinand von Wrangell was surveying the northern coast of the Chukotsk Peninsula (von Wrangell, 1840).

One other Russian expedition, under the command of Captain Fedor P. Lütke, was under way at the time of Captain Beechey's voyage on the *Blossom*. Lütke was ordered to explore the coasts of Kamchatka, Anadyr Gulf, Bering Strait and other places in the Pacific Ocean and Sea of Okhotsk (Lütke, 1835: I, ix-xiii). He circumnavigated the world from 1826 to 1829 in the sloop *Seniavine*, and in 1828—the year after Beechey left Bering Strait—he carried out detailed explorations on the Siberian coast of the strait.

After Beechey's voyage, foreign contacts and changes came quickly to the Eskimos of northwestern Alaska. The Russian-American Company established a trading post at St. Michael in 1833. In that same year a Russian, Tebenkov, traded on the south shore of Seward Peninsula as far as King Island (Burch, n.d.). Four years later the Russian-American Company's trading post at Unalakleet was set up, and Thomas Simpson of the Hudson's Bay Company reached Point Barrow in a boat by way of the Mackenzie River. In 1838 Alexander Kashevarov, an employee of the Russian-American Company, rounded Point Barrow from

Plate I Lithograph by Louis Choris of Eskimos of Kotzebue Sound, 1816. By courtesy of the British Museum.

Bering Strait. L. A. Zagoskin, also with the Russian-American Company, reached Norton Sound in 1842, and in 1842 and 1843 a ship from the same company, the *Okhotsk*, passed north of Bering Strait. In 1848 an American whaling captain, prompted by Beechey's report of large numbers of whales in the Arctic Ocean, reached Bering Strait and quickly took a large catch. The enormous success enjoyed by a few ships in the next year quickly drew others, and within a few years as many as 150 ships were passing into the Arctic Ocean annually. Point Barrow was reached by the whaling ships in 1854, and thereafter the Arctic fishery became an important seasonal activity. Along with the whalers came increasing numbers of trading vessels, and from 1848 to 1854 nine ships visited or wintered in the Bering Strait region and northern Alaska while searching for the missing expedition of Sir John Franklin.

Development of the Beechey Expedition

With the cessation of the Napoleonic wars the energies of the Royal Navy were channelled into surveying and exploration, and one objective of these efforts was the discovery of a northwest passage connecting the Atlantic and Pacific oceans. As a result, a profoundly scientific air characterizes all the journals of Arctic exploration published from the third through the sixth decade of the nineteenth century, and Gough has called attention to the emergent middle-class interest in the development of scientific knowledge as one of its causes. He notes that "the aims of science and empire were essentially one and the same" (Gough, 1973:4). Thus, while science was being advanced, the Lords of the Admiralty were not blind to the usefulness of accurate charts and surveys for possible future military operations. The Crown was sensitive also to Russia's activities in North America and the North Pacific, just as Russia was sensitive to England's activities in that area. The Secretary of the Admiralty, Sir John Barrow, aware that the Russians were interested in a northwest passage to the Atlantic, outfitted four expeditions to explore for it in the years 1818 and 1819. He wrote in 1817:

> The Russians have for some time been strongly impressed with the idea of an open passage round America. . . . It would be somewhat mortifying if a naval power but of yesterday should complete a discovery in the nineteenth century, which was so happily commenced by Englishmen in the Sixteenth. (Kirwan, 1960:77)

These British efforts were not wholly successful, but they did serve to delineate the land masses in the area where a northwest passage might be found, and because of this Barrow worried that Russia might capitalize on British discoveries. In 1823 John Franklin, one of the officers involved in the exploratory parties, proposed an expedition overland, down the Mackenzie River in boats to the sea and then west to Bering Strait, where the party could be met by a ship to bring it home (Gough, 1973:11). This idea was well received and was soon acted on by the Admiralty.

While the Admiralty was preparing its plans for exploration, Russia, worried about the activities of Great Britain and the United States in the Arctic area, began negotiating with its two rivals on the issue of Alaska's boundaries. The result was that in 1824 and 1825 Russia signed treaties first with the United States and then with Great Britain that defined the territorial limits of Alaska. Both countries thus formally recognized that Russia's boundaries in North America began in the east at the 141st meridian and extended from lat. 54°40′ N. to the Arctic Ocean. The treaty benefited the United States and Great Britain by permitting them to carry out trading and fishing operations for a decade in areas not being exploited by Russia (International Boundary Commission, [1918]:202-11). Hence, although Russia won a tactical victory in gaining the formal foreign recognition of Alaska's boundaries, in all practicality the advantage was lost (Foote, 1965:71-72).

In the 1820's the Hudson's Bay Company—a British counterpart to the Russian-American Company in aiming to extend territorial interests—supported the idea of the Royal Navy's expeditions which it hoped might block Russian expansion and competition. The outcome of this British concern was that in 1825 the Admiralty despatched Franklin overland and sent a naval force under the command of Captain William Edward Parry to attempt to sail through the Northwest Passage from the Atlantic to the Pacific. The Franklin and Parry expeditions were to rendezvous in Kotzebue Sound with another ship sent to meet them via the Pacific.

As early as 1824 the Russians learned of the plans for the British expedition, and they had not been idle: In that year Count Rumiantsev, who had financed von Kotzebue's explorations, planned a joint expedition with the Russian-American Company, under the leadership of Khromchenko, to complete von Kotzebue's and Shishmarev's surveys (Ray, n.d.*a.*). Rumiantsev wrote, "If it will happen that both expeditions will meet, then the glory of this undertaking will belong both to Russia and England. On the other hand if Russia will do nothing and the English will reach Bering Strait, Europe will be right in criticizing us for letting other nations do the exploration work in our seas and on our coast when our Asiatic and American possessions are in such close proximity" (Tikhmenev, 1939-40, I:335). Judging from the scope of Russian geographical knowledge at that time, it might have been an important and productive voyage, but it never occurred because of Rumiantsev's death (Ray, n.d.*a.*).

The Voyage of the Blossom: Its Preparation, Participants, and Results

Commander Frederick William Beechey was chosen as the person to bring H.M.S. *Blossom* to rendezvous with Franklin and Parry. His orders were to await the arrival of Franklin and Parry in Kotzebue Sound in 1826, and, should they not arrive then, to go south for the winter and return to Alaska again in 1827 (Gough, 1973:18; Ritchie, 1967:147-56).

The *Blossom* began to be prepared for her Arctic voyage in July 1824. Her hull was strengthened for the ice it would encounter and in January 1825 Captain Beechey came aboard to supervise her fitting out. A schooner-rigged barge was built for coastal surveys and various navigational and surveying instruments were included in the equipment (Gough, 1973:20-22). In addition, goods were carried for trading with natives along the route. The trade items were intended primarily for procuring food supplies, but it is probable that Beechey used some of the items to purchase ethnographic specimens. Among the objects he requested to be carried were

> 50 yards of blue and red broadcloth, iron in the form of hoops and bars, 500 hatchets, nails, saws, 4 cases of beads, jewellery and trinkets of different colours but mainly blue, 500 knives, 100 printed handkerchiefs, 50 kaleidoscopes, 100 bundles of needles, 40 pair of scissors, 80 looking glasses, 36 common shirts, 1,000 fish hooks of different sizes, [and] 10 bundles of vermilion. . . . (Gough, 1973:22)

In May, 1825 Beechey received his orders for the voyage; in addition to carrying out surveys in the Pacific Ocean and attempting to meet Franklin and Parry in Kotzebue Sound, he was to undertake a broad programme of scientific studies. It probably was under this section of his orders—to form collections of natural history specimens—that Beechey compiled his ethnographic materials. The orders from the Lords of the Admiralty stated:

> As we have appointed Mr. Tradescant Lay as naturalist on the voyage, and some of your officers are acquainted with certain branches of natural history, it is expected that your visits to numerous islands of the Pacific will afford the means of collecting rare and curious specimens in the several departments of this branch of science. You are to cause it to be understood that two specimens, *at least*, of each article are to be reserved for the public museums; after which the naturalist and officers will be at liberty to collect for themselves. . . . (Beechey, 1831, I:xii)

For the most part, the officers of the *Blossom* seem to have been an able group, and several of them deserve mention because of the ethnographic information found in their journals and records. Frederick William Beechey left the most comprehensive and well-written account of the ship's voyage. He seems to have been a conscientious and capable commander. His thorough, scientific mind may be seen in the breadth of his ethnographic collection, which is remarkable for its comprehensiveness in a time when artefacts were regarded more as curiosities than as objects of scientific value.

Beechey entered the Royal Navy in 1806 and in 1815 was promoted to Lieutenant for his participation in a boat operation on the lower Mississippi River during war with the United States. In 1818 he served on his first Arctic expedition aboard H.M.S. *Trent* under the command of John Franklin (Laughton, 1885); in 1819 he again went to the Arctic on H.M.S. *Hecla* under William Edward Parry, and on August 7, 1820, he became the first European to discover Banks Island (Parry, 1821:237). He rose to the rank of Commander in 1822, and three years later was put in command of H.M.S. *Blossom*. While still on the *Blossom* he was promoted to Captain. In 1834 he was given H.M.S. *Sulphur* for a surveying voyage in the Pacific, but ill health forced his resignation of the post a year later, and he was succeeded by Edward Belcher. Beechey spent the next decade surveying on the coast of Ireland, and in 1855 he was elected President of the Royal Geographical Society (Laughton, 1885).

Little is known of the life of Beechey's First Lieutenant, George Peard. From his journal, which is an interesting day-to-day chronicle, he appears a competent and thorough executive. He was in charge of many of the daily scientific duties of the expedition (Gough, 1973:50-54). Peard's solid, if colourless, account stands in marked contrast to that of Edward Belcher.

Belcher, who held the rank of Lieutenant, was listed on the *Blossom*'s rolls as supernumerary and assistant surveyor. He was "an able if disagreeable officer" according to Gough (1973:24), and, as described by Ritchie (1967:258-59) he "was active, intelligent, bombastic, querulous, warlike and forthright. He quarrelled with his seniors and abused his juniors". Born of a family of Loyalists who had emigrated from New England to Nova Scotia, Belcher moved with them to England and entered the Navy in 1812. His first important duty was aboard the *Blossom*. He was next put in command of H.M.S. *Aetna*, surveying on the west coast of Africa, and on his return from that voyage he was charged by his officers with harsh treatment of the crew. In 1836 Belcher replaced Captain Beechey on H.M.S. *Sulphur* when the Captain's poor health forced his return to England. At the completion of his mission Belcher was decorated and knighted, but again he was charged with having ill-treated his crew. In 1852 he was given the command of five ships participating in the Arctic search for the lost expedition of Sir John Franklin. The ships were eventually beset in the ice in the Arctic archipelago of Canada. Belcher ordered their abandonment in 1854 and returned home in his supply ships. He was court martialled for this action and acquitted, but he suffered much criticism, especially after one of the ships was found to have drifted free of the ice and was taken to the United States by an American whaling ship (Stuart-Stubbs, 1972:42-43).

Nor was Belcher's private life free from controversy. In 1833, after three years of marriage, his wife refused to live with him on the grounds that he had twice infected her with venereal disease. "Then began a protracted legal struggle which Belcher spitefully prolonged. Despite the bitterness of the separation, his wife was content to call herself Lady Belcher after Belcher was knighted a decade later" (Stuart-Stubbs, 1972:42).

Despite his shortcomings, Belcher was a useful officer. His moods and irascibility show clearly in the pages of his journal, yet these did not cloud his scientific interest or careful eye for ethnographic detail. Belcher's ethnographic collections at Oxford and in the British Museum equal the breadth of Beechey's, and the number of fine specimens reflects his

12

discernment as a collector. Perhaps it was his keen collector's instinct which, when frustrated, fuelled his animosity toward his Captain:

> About this time the Captain issued an order preventing the purchase of any thing unless shown to him to ascertain whether he chose to detain it for Government (or truly himself) and after this always prevented any officer purchasing from the [umiaks] until he and his minions had completely weeded them of everything worth having. (Belcher, n.d.:30).

Beechey does not, incidentally, appear to have reciprocated this animosity.

Admiralty Mate James Wolfe and Midshipman Richard Beechey, the captain's nephew, also kept journals that have survived (Plate II). They are lively and detailed accounts written by young men who found the Arctic regions both interesting and exciting. Although only fifteen years of age at the time of his writing, Richard Beechey gave a very full and enjoyable account of daily events, and his youthful enthusiasm radiates from the pages—a welcome change from the more sober journals of his superiors. Unfortunately, only a part of his journal remains.

The journals of the *Blossom*'s Master, Thomas Elson, and Mate, William Smyth, have probably not survived, but each was quoted in detail—by Peard in the former case and by Captain Beechey, Wolfe and Richard Beechey in the latter—for the most part concerning the operations of the *Blossom*'s barge in 1826. Each journal appears to have been a competent day-to-day account, with interesting information about encounters with the natives. The quotations of Elson and Smyth are of much historical importance because the barge, under the command of Elson, travelled unaccompanied from Point Franklin, through heavy ice and along unknown shores, until it discovered Point Barrow, the northernmost point of land in the western American Arctic.

John Bechervaise, a petty officer aboard the *Blossom*, also wrote a short account of the voyage in his memoirs (Lada-Mocarski, 1969:366). This book may have been written as much as ten years after the Blossom's return to England and therefore is of less value than the more precise daily records kept by other members of the expedition. Bechervaise did, however, note

Plate II James Wolfe's sketch of Eskimos offering trade goods. By courtesy of Yale University.

some details, which appear to be accurate, of the natives he encountered north of Bering Strait ([Bechervaise], 1839).

Although Captain Beechey himself certainly purchased many items for his ethnographic collections, he may have been assisted, for better or for worse, by at least three other officers of the ship: its naturalist, George Tradescant Lay; surgeon, Alexander Collie; and clerk, Charles Osmer.[1] Collie and Osmer helped him to compile an Eskimo vocabulary (Beechey, 1831, II:619), but Lay, whose duty it was to carry out scientific work and compile natural history collections, neglected his duty. During the first summer in the Arctic, Lay was left in the Hawaiian Islands, and Collie assumed his responsibilities (Beechey, 1831, I:233-34). Beechey twice reported the situation to the Admiralty:

> I have to acquaint their lordships that I have repeatedly demanded of Mr. Lay lists of the specimens which have been collected, but he has not furnished me with any.[2]

> To Mr. Collie the surgeon the service is indebted for his assiduity in collecting specimens of various kinds, and for the willingness with which, during the absence of Mr. Lay he conducted the duties of his departments.[3]

The *Blossom* left England in May 1825 and proceeded via Rio de Janeiro around Cape Horn, reaching Valparaiso, Chile, in October. From there the ship sailed west to the Tuamotu Archipelago, carrying out surveys and discovering some new islands. Pitcairn Island was visited, and there the officers interviewed the last survivor of the *Bounty* mutiny. The *Blossom* then stopped at Tahiti, Honolulu and Petropavlovsk on the Kamchatka Peninsula, and there Beechey heard of the return of Captain Parry's expedition. The ship then continued north,

Plate III Detail of watercolour sketch of the *Blossom* with umiaks at St. Lawrence Island, July 17th, 1826. Reproduced with the sanction of Controller of H.M.S.O. and the Hydrographer of the navy.

reached St. Lawrence Island (Plate III) and was visited by the natives there before it continued on into Kotzebue Sound on July 22, 1826. Three days later it arrived at Chamisso Island, the designated point for the rendezvous with Franklin. No sign of Franklin was found, so Beechey set about a series of explorations of the immediate area with the ship's barge, and Hotham Inlet was discovered. Beechey then took the *Blossom* northward in company with the barge, parallel to the coast, and stops were made at several places to erect beacons on shore for Franklin. Together the two vessels reached Point Franklin.

Later, near Icy Cape, the barge, under the command of Elson, was sent northward alone to explore the coast and search for Franklin while the *Blossom* returned to Kotzebue Sound. The

---

[1] Collie and Osmer also kept journals, but apparently these have not survived (F. W. Beechey, Letters Incoming, Miscellaneous Papers, page 6, AD5 (II), Vol. 58, Archives, Hydrographic Department, Ministry of Defence (N), Taunton, Somerset).

[2] Beechey to John Wilson Croker 29 April 1827 from Macao; Public Record Office, class ADM 1, box 1576, number B40.

[3] Beechey to John Barrow 4 October 1828 from Woolwich; Public Record Office, class ADM 1, box 1576, number B198.

barge succeeded in reaching Point Barrow and in charting more than one hundred miles of previously unrecorded coast. Elson was able to stay at Point Barrow only a short time, however, because of the hostile appearance and superior numbers of natives there. On retracing his track southward, he encountered difficulties with heavy ice along Skull Cliff but was able to return safely to the ship at Kotzebue Sound. The reason why Elson's party did not make contact with Franklin was that five days before Elson reached Point Barrow, Franklin reached his farthest point westward, Return Reef, near the Colville River, and from there he had returned to the Mackenzie River. Franklin had reached a point within 150 miles of Elson's farthest point and this meant that in 1826 the coastal areas between Return Reef and Point Barrow, with the coast between Coppermine River and Fury and Hecla Strait, remained the last uncharted shores of continental North America (Gough, 1973:39). Through the expeditions of Franklin and Beechey the British had significantly extended their territorial knowledge in northern North America—a sharp riposte to Russia's advances.

In mid-October 1826 Beechey sailed out of the Arctic and headed for San Francisco, intent on renewing his search for Franklin in 1827. From California the *Blossom* crossed the Pacific Ocean to Honolulu and Macao and in the spring arrived at Petropavlovsk where Beechey surveyed and sounded the harbour, gaining information that was of value to the Anglo-French fleet during its abortive expeditions against that town during the Crimean War. The *Blossom* anchored off Cape Rodney on August 2, 1827, and the barge, under Elson, was put out to carry on with its coastal surveys. Beechey wanted to explore the coast between Cape Rodney and Cape Prince of Wales and, in particular, to check on reports that a large bay existed south of Bering Strait. Elson reached the *Blossom* at Chamisso Island nine days later and reported finding a large harbour to the southeast of Cape Prince of Wales.

While at Chamisso Island the crew of the *Blossom* buried a supply of flour and beads for Franklin (Plate IV). This cache was discovered later, in 1849 when H.M.S. *Herald*, H.M.S. *Plover* and the yacht, *Nancy Dawson* were searching for Franklin's missing third expedition. Captain Henry Kellett (H.M.S. *Herald*) fed the ships' officers on pies and puddings made from the flour (Ritchie, 1967:258-59).

Beechey then took the *Blossom* north in company with the barge, this time under the command of Belcher. Encountering heavy ice near Icy Cape, Beechey returned to the south while the barge kept on to the north, close to shore. Beechey took the *Blossom* first to Chamisso Island and then through Bering Strait to the harbour that Elson had reported. This body of water was surveyed and named Port Clarence in honour of the Duke of Clarence (Map 6). The *Blossom* then returned to Chamisso Island and found Belcher camped on shore. He reported that the barge had been able to travel only a short distance beyond Icy Cape and that, returning, it had been wrecked off the shore of Choris Peninsula in a sudden gale that caused the deaths of three of the crew. During the gale several Eskimos had been present on shore and had refused to go to the rescue of the men on the foundering barge after the heavy seas had repeatedly driven their boat back to shore. Some ill-will was felt by the British at this incident, perhaps without justification, and also at the ensuing pilfering of the barge's wreckage. Shortly thereafter hostilities broke out when the aggressive behaviour of another group of Eskimos resulted in the wounding of three sailors and the death of one Eskimo. The dead man was the first Eskimo reported killed by a European in northwestern Alaska (Foote, 1965:85).

This unfortunate incident occurred in the face of otherwise friendly encounters between the natives and members of the *Blossom*'s crew. The British, fully aware of the vulnerability of the Franklin's small party, took pains to establish good relations with the Eskimos. This may explain why the sailors collected so much information about the natives and why such a large amount of ethnographic material was purchased. Wolfe wrote that in 1826 at Cape Thompson,

Plate IV Beads of the type used by Beechey to purchase artefacts. Buried at Chamisso Island by the crew of *H.M.S. Blossom* for Sir John Franklin. By courtesy of the Royal Geographical Society.

Map 6. Detail of Beechey's Chart of Port Clarence

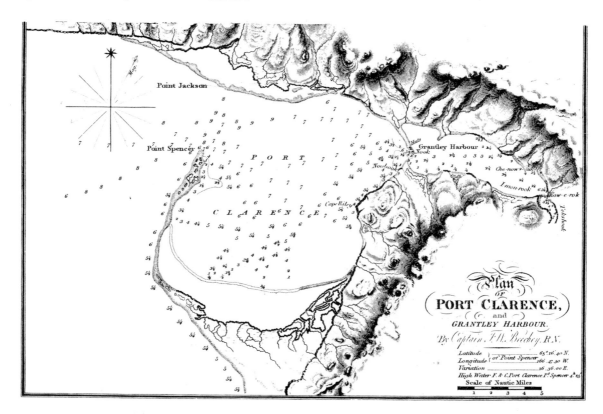

"During our stay we purchased almost everything there was in the village disposable, more for the sake of their gratification than our own" (Wolfe, n.d.:119).

In early October the fast-approaching freeze-up of Kotzebue Sound forced Beechey to leave the Arctic. The ship visited California, Mexico, and Chile, and then rounded Cape Horn. After a stop in Rio de Janeiro, it arrived in England in October 1828.

Although Beechey failed to contact Franklin, the expedition was of consequence both cartographically and scientifically. A large number of natural history collections and scientific studies were made in the Arctic, and they resulted in several important publications.[4] Beechey's contributions were also significant from the standpoint of ethnography for they have provided the factual basis for much subsequent research. In addition to collecting objects of material culture, Beechey made and recorded careful observations about the Eskimos. An Eskimo vocabulary was compiled at Kotzebue Sound, and it was through this medium that Beechey correctly delineated the dialectical border on Norton Sound dividing the Yupik- and Inupik-speaking Eskimo groups (Beechey, 1831, II:576).

Beechey holds the distinction of being the first man to identify the natives of northwestern Alaska as Eskimos. Only Captain Cook (*Beaglehole, 1967, I:468*), and John Ledyard (1963: 86) before him had speculated that the natives of Alaska resembled Eskimos. Beechey, however, unlike Captain Cook, had the benefit of being able to compare his observations with the excellent ethnographic information gathered in northern Hudson Bay and the Foxe Basin during Captain Parry's second Arctic expedition in 1821-23. Furthermore, some of the men who had sailed with Parry were aboard the *Blossom*. Wolfe wrote, "Those on board who had been on the NW Expedition with Captain Parry recognized . . . a great similarity with their former acquaintance." "That they are the same race with the Esquimaux there can be no doubt, their round chubby face and small features alone would suffice to prove it, were it not for the resemblance in language, manners, dress, which served as a confirmation" (Wolfe, n.d.:110). He added later, "The general remark was 'Precisely the same people, but two of the girls are not bad looking'. Chacun à son goût." (Wolfe, n.d.:122).

Cartographically, the voyage was no less a success. Today, of course, much of the coast of northern Alaska is distinguished by Beechey's and Franklin's nomenclature. Some of the names Beechey chose are well known: Elson Lagoon, Point Barrow, Cape Smyth, Peard Bay, Sea Horse Islands, Point Franklin, Point Belcher, Wainwright Inlet, Blossom Shoals, Point Lay, Cape Beaufort, Point Hope, Cape Thompson, Cape Seppings, Hotham Inlet, Cape Blossom, Buckland River, Cape York, Point Spencer, Port Clarence and Grantley Harbor. It is interesting that both Beechey and Franklin named geographical features after the famous Professor of Geology at Oxford, the Rev. Dr. William Buckland, F.R.S. Beechey named a river after him at Eschscholtz Bay, near the place where he collected the bones of Pleistocene mammals that Buckland later described in an appendix to Beechey's narrative. Franklin gave Buckland's name to a range of mountains in Alaska close to the Arctic Ocean and near the border of the Yukon Territory of Canada. Beechey and Franklin also independently honoured one another at about the same date in 1826. Point Franklin and Beechey Point lie near the extreme points of land each man reached.

The naming of various landmarks may have been prompted by more than mere honorary considerations; international politics were perhaps equally, if not more, important. Some of the places named by Beechey north of Kotzebue Sound had already been charted by Vasiliev and Shishmarev during their explorations of 1820 and 1821, and Beechey was aware of these previous explorations. Point Hope and Cape Thompson had been named respectively Capes

[4] See, for instance, Richardson (1839) and Hooker (1841).

Golovnin and Rikord by Vasiliev and Shishmarev; when describing Cape Thompson, Beechey mentioned that "a cape close to this had been named Cape Ricord by the Russians" (Beechey, 1831, I:262). This is a puzzling statement because Cape Thompson is a discrete headland. Later in 1826 when a post was found on Chamisso Island bearing the names of von Kotzebue's and Vasiliev's ships, Beechey, although in error about the ships' commanders, remarked that he assumed Shishmarev had carved it during his voyage of 1820 (Beechey, 1831, I:286). Richard Beechey wrote that "this was unintelligible to all on board though by some of the letters in the first word resembling Greek, the number and date we considered that it must have been intended for [von Kotzebue's ship]. The latter was supposed to have been done by a vessel which we knew had been here since" (Richard Beechey, n.d.:80). And yet before this incident Captain Beechey, near Point Franklin, had written, "We were not conscious of any other vessel having been upon the coast since Kotzebue's voyage" (Beechey, 1831, I:274). By 1822, at the latest, Cape Golovnin (Point Hope) had appeared on charts published in Paris (Choris, 1822); nevertheless if the British had not previously learned about recent Russian Arctic explorations, they surely would have learned about them when the *Blossom* visited Petropavlovsk in 1826. Both Baron von Wrangell and the Governor of Kamchatka, whom Beechey met there, would have known of the voyages that followed von Kotzebue's expedition (Belcher, n.d.:18).

Nevertheless, by 1827 the British had received recent Russian charts of the Bering Strait region. In 1827, while on the barge approaching Port Clarence, Wolfe wrote that despite heavy weather setting in, "We did not however hesitate in running as from a recent chart by Schischmareff corroborated by intelligence obtained from the natives we had reason to expect an Inlet which we trusted would at least afford shelter to our little schooner from the approaching gale" (Wolfe, n.d.:195)[5]. And Belcher mentioned that, "Owing to very bad weather the Master had run into an inlet marked in the Russian Charts which he found very capacious and a very eligible harbour" (Belcher, n.d.:182).[6]

Evidence thus indicates that Beechey knew of prior Russian explorations north of Kotzebue Sound and that he possessed a map by Shishmarev. His apparently deliberate ignorance of the Russians' precedence in the area suggests a political manoeuvre: Beechey's and Franklin's surveys and nomenclature could have been used to provide a basis for the extension of British territorial claims on the lands from north of Kotzebue Sound to the Mackenzie River.

[5] In 1826 natives at Chamisso Island sketched for Beechey a map of the area, which included Port Clarence (p. 000). Beechey remarked in his narrative that this instance was the first he had learned of Port Clarence. (Beechey, 1831:I, 291). If one assumes this statement to be correct, then Beechey may have received a copy of Shishmarev's map when he visited Petropavlovsk in 1827.

[6] It is probable that the Russians, like the British, had received information about the size and character of Port Clarence and adjacent regions from native informants. The "recent chart by Schischmareff" (Wolfe, n.d.:195) which Beechey possessed, probably contained the same information as that which appeared by 1824 in a Russian Admiralty chart (Yefimov, 1964: Plate 191) and in the later version of Sarychev's Atlas (1826:Plate 4). Sarychev's chart of the Bering Strait region (plate 4) delineates with fair accuracy the shores of Port Clarence and nearby waters. This information may have been passed on by Khromchenko, for whom a native had drawn a map of the Port Clarence area in 1822 (Ray, n.d. *a.*).

The British apparently believed that no Europeans had previously visited Port Clarence, because Elson wrote that "it's supposed not to be known before I discovered it in August, 1827". (Thomas Elson, Letters Incoming, Miscellaneous Papers, page 274.AD5 (II), Vol. 58, Hydrographic Department, Ministry of Defence (N), Taunton, Somerset.)

I am indebted to Dorothy Jean Ray for her helpful suggestions on this matter.

THE COLLECTIONS

The Beechey and Belcher collections have travelled different routes on their way to the Pitt Rivers Museum at Oxford and each collection, on the whole, is disappointing with regard to records of provenance. It has not been possible to determine whether records covering the acquisition of ethnographic items were kept by Beechey or Belcher because no evidence has been found in the several archival sources of Oxford University, or in records of the Royal Navy at the Public Record Office, or in records of the Hydrographer of the Navy, or in the British Museum, or in a number of other archival and record collections. In the descriptions of the artefacts listed in this volume, therefore, it has been impossible to attribute the place or date of collection to many of the pieces.

The first listing of Beechey's collection at Oxford appears in the 1836 catalogue of the Ashmolean Museum (Ashmolean Museum, 1836:185-87); nevertheless, the gift to the Museum may have been made as early as 1828 because in December of that year Beechey donated several of his Eskimo artefacts to the British Museum. It may have been Beechey's high regard for Parry—and for the ethnographical descriptions recorded on Parry's second voyage to the Eastern Arctic—that prompted Beechey to give his collection to the Ashmolean, where a large number of artefacts collected on Parry's voyage were already housed. In his *Narrative of a Voyage to the Pacific and Bering's Strait* Beechey frequently drew on the journal Parry published in 1828 to make comparative descriptions of the Eskimos.

The Ashmolean's catalogue of 1836 lists the earliest records of provenance for Oxford's collections of Beechey's artefacts. In some cases the exact place of purchase is noted, and it would seem that these assignations are largely trustworthy, judging from Beechey's accurate recording of information in other scientific matters. In most cases, however, the objects are labelled merely "Esquimaux", and although typologically they are certainly from the western Arctic, many cannot be designated more precisely than as having come from the broad area that Beechey and his crew visited: that is, the coastal area from St. Lawrence Island to Point Barrow.

In 1886 the Beechey Collection was transferred to the Pitt Rivers Museum along with most of the Ashmolean's ethnological material. Here, in accord with General Pitt Rivers' schema, the items were grouped in categories according to function rather than according to their culture area. The Beechey and Belcher collections were reunited and assembled as a unit from one cultural area in 1973.

It is probable that Belcher, who made his collection privately, retained the artefacts in his possession until some time near his death in 1877. Belcher sold a large number of his ethnological specimens in 1872, and part of the British Museum's Belcher collection was acquired from the sale. It is probable that General Pitt Rivers also bought some of Belcher's artefacts at that time.

The fact that Belcher's collection was transferred to the Pitt Rivers Collection at a late date—possibly as many as fifty years after the *Blossom*'s voyage—seems to account for the inaccurate record of provenance in a number of cases. Most of the Eskimo artefacts in the Belcher collection were recorded by Belcher as having come from Icy Cape. Although Belcher certainly stopped at Icy Cape in 1827 when he was in command of the *Blossom*'s barge, his journal records the purchase of items at other points on the coast both in 1826 and in 1827. It seems, then, that his designations should be viewed with some scepticism.

Further doubt is cast on the accuracy of Belcher's designations by the presence of a few items in both the Pitt Rivers and British Museums' Collections that are demonstrably wrongly labelled. Some of these most probably were purchased on the Pacific coast of Alaska in the

1830s when Belcher visited there in H.M.S. *Sulphur*, and others, undoubtedly from northwestern Alaska, are labelled as having come from the eastern Arctic during Belcher's ill-fated participation in the search for Sir John Franklin. These inaccuracies all seem to stem from the late date at which the collection was apparently transferred to the Pitt Rivers collection. It is also regrettable that during the last century and a half a small number of objects in the collections has been lost. This most probably was the result of several relocations and rather casual curatorial care in the nineteenth century. Most of the objects that have survived are in good condition.

The writings of several Arctic ethnographers have been very useful in preparing the descriptions of objects in the Beechey and Belcher collections. It is fortunate that northwestern Alaska was an area in which two of the most thorough and enterprising Arctic ethnographers—John Murdoch and Edward Nelson—carried out their work. From 1877 to 1881 Nelson was based at St. Michael, near the mouth of the Yukon River, carrying out meteorological observations, but he ranged both north and south of there collecting ethnographic information and artefacts. His primary work, *The Eskimo About Bering Strait* (1899), deals for the most part with the Eskimos near the Yukon River, Norton Sound and the immediate region near Bering Strait. Murdoch, a member of the International Polar Expedition, lived at Point Barrow from 1881 to 1883. He wrote detailed information about the natives of that area in the *Ethnological Results of the Point Barrow Expedition* (1892).

The Eskimos of Alaska who populate the area from Norton Bay to Beechey Point on the Beaufort Sea have close linguistic affiliations and a high degree of homogeneity in their material culture. Most of the Beechey and Belcher collections were made in this area and the objects described in the present catalogue have for the most part been compared with other collections from this area. Occasionally, however, it has been useful to extend the comparisons to groups south of the Yukon River delta and to groups east of the Mackenzie River delta as far as the Coronation Gulf area. In the latter area live the Copper Eskimos, a group not closely related to the Eskimos of northwestern Alaska. In the early twentieth century the Copper Eskimos were visited by Diamond Jenness and Vilhjalmur Stefansson, two skilled ethnographers—who were among the first Europeans to meet these people—and their observations are in some ways comparable to those made by members of the *Blossom*'s crew.

The artefacts described in the following pages are grouped largely according to functional classifications. Each artefact is listed, first with this catalogue's number and then by a notation indicating whether it is part of the Beechey collection or the Belcher collection. The Pitt Rivers Museum's accession number is next. The object's dimensions are then given, followed by a discussion of the salient features of the piece. Where appropriate, general remarks concerning the item are included. Photographs of each specimen are included with the text and the figure numbers are shown in brackets. Photographs of catalogue numbers 49 and 50 are not included. The catalogue numbers have been shown in the photographs depicting more than one specimen.

HUNTING AND FISHING EQUIPMENT

Bows

The strength and construction of the Eskimo sinew-backed bow has impressed western observers from Frobisher's time on (Hakluyt, 1589:628); in fact, most of the surviving accounts of the *Blossom*'s voyage tell of crew members' seeing an Eskimo at Kotzebue Sound shoot an arrow through the eye of a loon at a distance estimated at from 20 to 40 yards. Stefansson, on the other hand, who witnessed the Copper Eskimos using similar bows, estimated that 25 to 30 yards was the maximum range of great accuracy, but stated that the bow was effective on caribou at 75 to 90 yards. He pointed out, though, that at 35 to 50 yards an arrow could pass through the body of a caribou (Stefansson, 1914:96). Belcher (1861:139) reported that the extreme range of the bow was as much as 176 yards.

Stefansson (1914:89) stated that Copper Eskimos favoured the leg sinew of an old bull caribou for the backing of their bows—leg sinew is coarser than back sinew (Jenness, 1946:87)—while Eskimos of the Mackenzie River delta used beluga (*Delphinapterus leucas*) sinew, which was probably as strong (Stefansson, 1914:379).

Sinew strengthening cables required a certain amount of care. Because sinew stretches when damp, the bow would have been carried in a waterproof bag (Murdoch, 1892:207-09; Stefansson, 1914:96). Stefansson (1914:96) noted that among the Copper Eskimos the tension on sinew-backed bows needed to be constantly checked and adjusted and that their bows were often taken apart and reconstructed.

In northern Alaska there is archaeological evidence for the use of both one-piece and three-piece bow frames. Frames have been found well preserved in the frozen middens near Point Barrow. Comparatively recently, bow frames used in that area were often made from a single piece of wood (Ford, 1959:22, fig. 4), but three-piece frames have been found in association with Birnirk cultural materials of about A.D. 500-800 (Ford, 1959:121, fig. 55*c*). A model of a single-piece bow frame, probably a child's toy, was found in an Ipiutak culture site (*ca.* A.D. 400) at Feniak Lake in the Brooks Range (Hall, n.d.) and fragments of a three-piece bow with V-splice joints have been found on the Jones Islands near the mouth of the Colville River, possibly dating to as early as A.D. 1550 (Irving, 1953:92, plate 3).

With the advent of firearms, the bow, unlike the harpoon, quickly became obsolete. Whymper (1869:169) reported that in 1867 at Port Clarence, where Chukchees, Eskimos and whalers met to trade, a large proportion of the natives had flintlock and percussion cap guns and that bows were not in wide use. As contact between whites and Eskimos increased in more remote areas the use of bows became more and more restricted. By the early 1880s, at Point Barrow, they were used only for the taking of birds and as children's toys (Murdoch, 1892:195-96). According to Stefansson (1914:379) they were still in use in the area of the Mackenzie River delta in 1885. He reported that both one-piece and three-piece frames were used and that they were usually made from pieces of spruce with a suitable bend. In the area of Coronation Gulf and Victoria Island they were still being used by the Copper Eskimos when Stefansson and Jenness visited there in the second decade of this century. Their use ended shortly thereafter, however, when the fur trade became established in that region.

A drawing of a bow was included in Beechey's hydrographic sketches (Plate V). It appears to resemble bow number 3. Under the drawing, however, is the notation "from 2 ft. to 5". This is interesting for, other than suggesting that Beechey saw a variety of sizes of bows, it suggests that he may have viewed a *komiktak*, a small bow that was carried hidden under clothing and used by murderers to take their victims by surprise. This type was used with arrows of proportional size (Stefansson, 1914:390).

Bechervaise purchased a bow in the Tuksuk Channel near Port Clarence for a knife and two buttons ([Bechervaise], 1839:236)—a seemingly high price when compared to the price of other items purchased during the voyage; Beechey (1831:I, 210) was unable to purchase one at Point Lay for a brooch.

Beechey described having witnessed the manufacture of a bow frame: "It requires some care to bring a bow to the form which they consider best," he wrote, "and for this purpose they wrap it in shavings soaked in water, and hold it over a fire; it is then pegged down upon the earth in the form required" (Beechey, 1831:II, 575). Belcher also described the manufacturing process:

> Their bows are remarkably well made and evidence much ingenuity, the strength being in a very slight measure dependant on the wood, which is usually fir. . . .

> The wood is first steamed . . . and two pieces of bone and ivory fitted to the angle; twisted gut is then passed from end to end and hitched alternately . . . [the sinew reinforcement] acts as the sinews on the back of a snake so that the great strength of the bow is owing chiefly to these sinews on its back, and such is that it requires considerable strength to bend it more than would break the ordinary ones I have seen of other countries (Belcher, n.d.:26).

Belcher may have been the first to call attention to the similarities between the Eskimo and Asiatic composite bows: "It has always appeared to me that their object has been to produce a form very similar to the strung bow of the Tartars," he wrote, "and *totally dissimilar* to the tribes of the Indians on the American shores southerly" (Belcher, 1861:142).

Of the three bows in the Beechey and Belcher collections the lashings and sinew arrangements on numbers 1 and 2 (Figs. 1-2) closely resemble the arrangements on a specimen collected at Point Barrow in the 1880s (Murdoch, 1885; plate 4, fig. 9) and are similar to those on bows obtained farther to the east—from the Copper Eskimos around Coronation Gulf and from the Netsilik Eskimos of King William Island (Jenness, 1946:123, fig. 151, B right; Taylor, 1974:58). Hamilton (1970) has pointed out, however, that the recurve built into the *siyahs*, or "ears", of a frame like that of number 2 (Fig. 2) would give the bow a great advantage in thrust over a specimen similar to number 3 (Fig. 3) in which the *siyahs* are vestigial. Bow number 3 resembles one collected on the lower Yukon River between 1877 and 1881 (Murdoch, 1885: plate 5), and one collected at St. Michael in the 1890s (Edmonds, 1966:125). It also resembles, in general, a bow collected at Prince William Sound during Cook's voyage there (Bandi, 1956:fig. 6). Knowing that Belcher visited Prince William Sound in 1837 (Belcher, 1843) and that his record of provenance is occasionally inaccurate, it should not be ruled out that this bow could have been purchased from the Pacific Eskimos and was later wrongly labelled.

Descriptions of the three bows in the collections follow.

1. Beechey Collection, Museum no. A.M. 733
   Length, 122 cm.; width seen from front, 39 mm. near nocks and 32 mm. at centre; thickness, 17 mm. near nocks and 21 mm. at centre. According to the 1836 Ashmolean Museum Catalogue, collected northeast of Icy Cape. (Fig. 1, A-C).

The frame of this specimen is made from one piece of spruce, and it has antler chocks at the "knees", which apparently help to preserve the bow's curves. The backing is made of about thirty metres of three-strand caribou (*Rangifer tarandus*) sinew twine which is 2 mm. in diameter and probably in a single piece. In constructing the sinew backing, the twine was first

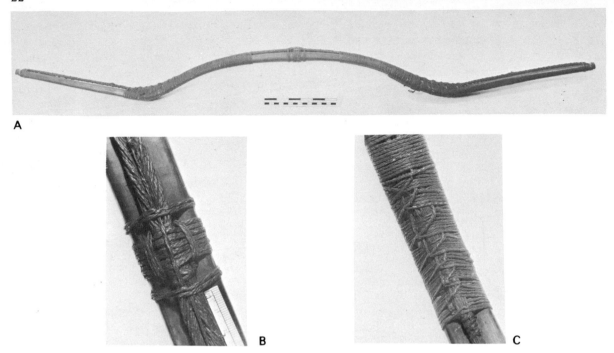

A

B   C

Fig. 1

wrapped from nock to nock approximately fifteen times; then the wrapping was continued in shorter lengths closer to the centre of the frame and the lashings were held with a series of half hitches. There are about nine of these shorter wrappings. Near the centre of the bow the twine is gathered into two cables of about twelve strands each. The cables could be twisted, in opposite directions, to increase tension on the bow's frame. At one point on the frame a piece of antler is lashed, apparently to reinforce a weakness. This specimen lacks a bowstring.

2. Beechey Collection, Museum no. A.M. 734
    Length on curve 138 cm.; length on chord 124 cm.; width seen from front 26 mm. near nocks, 39 mm. at "knees" and 30 mm. at centre; thickness 11 mm. near nocks and 26 mm. at centre. According to the 1836 Ashmolean Museum Catalogue collected from the Western Eskimo, northeast of Icy Cape. (Fig. 2)

    The frame of this bow is constructed of three pieces of spruce with V-splices at the joints. It has antler chocks at the "knees". The backing is composed of approximately thirty metres of

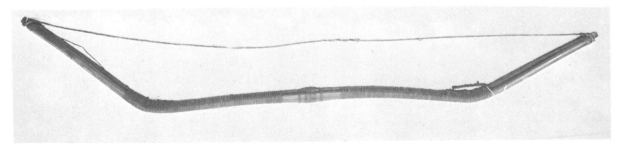

Fig. 2

three-strand caribou sinew about 1.5 mm. in thickness; it is wrapped and gathered in a manner similar to that of number 1. There is a strip of caribou skin along the back of the frame, under the sinew lashings, and there has been a secondary, reinforcing lashing at each "knee". The bowstring is approximately 120 cm. long and is made from one continuous piece of three-strand sinew twine, about 1.5 mm. in thickness and about fifteen metres long. In constructing the bowstring the twine was led from nock to nock about twelve times.

3. Belcher Collection, unnumbered.
   Length, 135 cm.; width seen from front, 28 mm. at centre and 52 mm. at widest; thickness, 15 mm. near nocks, 11 mm. at "knees" and 26 mm. at centre; antler strip is 62.7 cm. long by 11 mm. wide by 9 mm. thick. According to Pitt Rivers Museum Catalogue, possibly collected at Icy Cape. (Fig. 3, A-D)

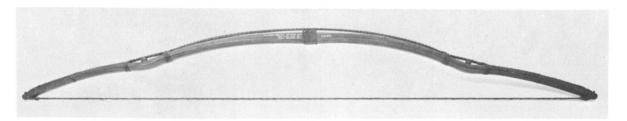

A

B

D   C

Fig. 3

The frame of this bow is made from one piece of spruce, and the backing strip is made of antler. The chocks at the "knees" are made from cylindrical pieces of wood, 13 mm. in diameter and 38 mm. long. The backing cable is made from about forty-five metres of three-strand caribou sinew, approximately 2 mm. in diameter. Like the other bows, the sinew twine was first passed from nock to nock about thirty times and then seized to the frame with half hitches in eight groupings, progressively closer toward the centre. The centre seizing was done with another piece of sinew twine. The bowstring was made from one continuous piece of three-strand, 2 mm. sinew twine about 11.5 metres long. It was constructed by first leading the twine from nock to nock and then by seizing and reinforcing the loops at each end.

Marlin Spikes (sinew adjusting implements)

Marlin spikes were part of a hunter's personal tool kit. They were used in the construction, repair and adjustment of the sinew backing on bows by prying up the sinew cables or opening their lay for the insertion of sinew twisting rods. Four types of marlin spikes are represented in the Beechey and Belcher collections (Fig. 4). Type 1 (Catalogue Numbers 4 and 5) and type 2 (Catalogue Numbers 6, 7 and 8) have central holes for attachment to a line. A pair of these could have been put on a line with two sinew twisting rods and, probably, an arrow fletcher. They would have been carried in the tool bag of a hunter, and the bag would have been attached to his quiver and bow bag to be readily at hand for adjustments in the field. Beechey illustrated one of these sets in his hydrographic sketches (Plate V). Types 1 and 2 are quite similar; their slight difference is in shape. Specimens similar to the type 2 spikes are represented in collections from the Point Barrow area (Murdoch, 1892:291, fig. 283), but, curiously enough, marlin spikes of the type 1 variety are not reported by ethnographers in that area. The type 3 marlin spike (Catalogue Number 9) is larger and lacks a lashing hole. This suggests that it was not an implement taken regularly into the field. A similar specimen, with a crustacean carved on the proximal end, was illustrated by Murdoch (1892:292, fig. 284) from the Point Barrow area. Its tip had been cut down to serve as an arrow fletcher. Type 4 (Catalogue Number 10) cannot be identified as solely a marlin spike. It may have served other

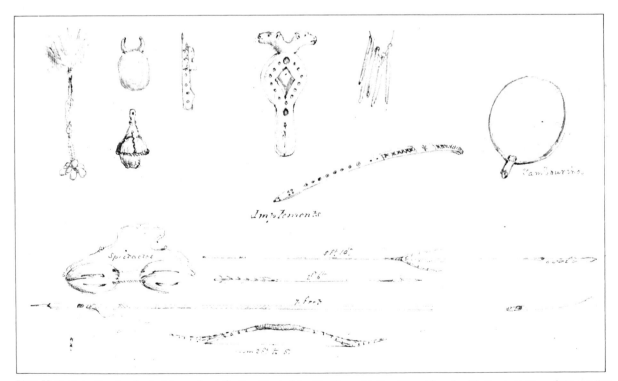

Plate V Captain Beechey's sketches of artefacts collected in Northern Alaska. Reproduced with the sanction of Controller H.M.S.O. and the Hydrographer of the Navy.

functions as well. Objects of general resemblance were observed in use as marlin spikes among the Copper Eskimos (Stefansson, 1914:94, fig. 39*a*) and as a woman's sewing implement and marrow extractor (Jenness, 1946:90-92).

The marlin spikes acquired by Beechey and Belcher are described below.

4. Beechey Collection, Museum no. A.M. 777
    Length, 9.7 cm.; diameter of hole drilled at centre, 1.mm.; walrus (*Odobenus rosmarus divergens*) ivory. (Fig. 4:4)

5. Beechey Collection, Museum no. A.M. 776
    Length, 10.2 cm.; diameter of hole drilled at centre, 2 mm.; walrus ivory. (Fig. 4:5)

6. Beechey Collection, Museum no. A.M. 774
    Length, 17.5 cm.; diameter of hole drilled at centre, 2 mm.; walrus ivory. (Fig. 4:6)

This marlin spike has incised lines running longitudinally on both sides.

7. Beechey Collection, probably Museum no. A.M. 775
    Length, 16.5 cm.; diameter of hole drilled at centre, 2 mm.; walrus ivory. (Fig. 4:7)

This specimen has incised lines running the length of both sides. On one side there is also an incised concentric circle-and-dot motif.

8. Belcher Collection, unnumbered.
    Length, 12.3 cm.; diameter of hole drilled at centre, 2 mm.; walrus ivory. (Fig. 4:8)

One side of this specimen has a finely incised line decoration, a portion of which has small dentates.

9. Belcher Collection, unnumbered.
    Length, 19.5 cm.; walrus ivory. According to Pitt Rivers Museum Catalogue collected at Icy Cape. (Fig. 5, A and B)

There is a representation of a human face carved on the proximal end of this implement. The eye holes have been drilled and small gouges on the cheeks represent labret holes.

10. Belcher Collection, unnumbered.
    Length, 15.6 cm.; walrus ivory. According to Pitt Rivers Museum Catalogue collected at Icy Cape. (Fig. 4:10)

Sinew Twisting Rods

Sinew twisting rods were used to adjust the tension of the sinew backing cables of a bow. They were inserted among the strands of the cable and were most often used in pairs to keep similar tension in both of the cables. In the tightening or loosening process, the marlin spike would first be forced among the strands to allow the entry of the twisting rod. When the leading end of the rod had passed through to the other side of the cable, its trailing end would be rotated 180°. The rod would then be pushed back through the cable and rotated another 180°; the process would be continued, with the rods "slipping back and forth, like the handle of a [carpenter's] vise" until properly adjusted (Murdoch, 1885:316; plate II).

26

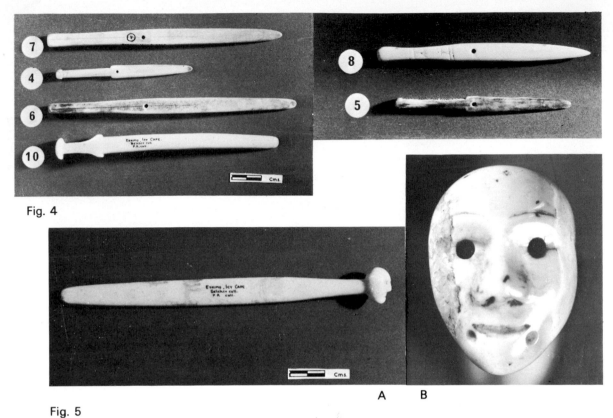

Fig. 4

Fig. 5

A   B

11. Beechey Collection, Museum no. A.M. 772
    Length, 12.0 cm.; drilled hole at centre, 2 mm. in diameter; walrus ivory. According to
    Pitt Rivers Museum Catalogue, collected in northwestern Alaska. (Fig. 6:11)

There is a shallow incised groove running the length of both the obverse and the reverse
sides.

12. Beechey Collection, probably Ashmolean Museum Catalogue no. A.M. 773
    Length, 12.0 cm.; drilled hole at centre, 2 mm. in diameter; walrus ivory. (Fig. 6:12)

This item is identical with number 11, and most probably they are a pair.

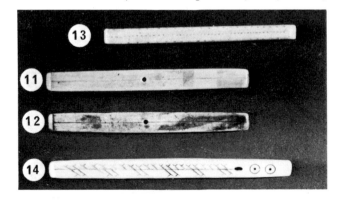

Fig. 6

13. Belcher Collection, Museum no. P.R. 19R
    Length, 11.5 cm.; walrus ivory. (Fig. 6:13)

Each side is ornamented with a line of deeply incised dots running parallel with the long axis.

14. Belcher Collection, Museum no. P.R. 19R
    Length, 14.4 cm.; walrus ivory. (Fig. 6:14)

There is a 5 mm. gouged hole near one end of this specimen. It is decorated with a lightly incised stalk-and-stem pattern and with two circles with centre dots.

Arrows

All arrow shafts in the Beechey and Belcher collections were made from spruce, which most probably came to the Eskimos as driftwood. In northwestern Alaska Eskimos made their arrow shafts of one piece of wood because driftwood was abundant in the areas they inhabited. Farther to the east, where wood was scarce, the Copper Eskimos often made arrow shafts from several short pieces of wood spliced together with lashings and seal-blood glue and then dried over a charcoal fire (Stefansson, 1914:91-92). Archaeological sites near Point Barrow contain single-piece arrow shafts in association with materials of the Birnirk culture (*ca.* A.D. 500-800). The ends of these arrows are often charred, probably because the arrows were used secondarily as wick trimmers for lamps (Ford, 1959:122-23).

Stefansson (1914:392) reported that the length of arrow shafts made by Point Barrow and Utukok River Eskimos was in proportion to the archer's size: the shaft was equal to the distance from the sternum to the second thumb joint when held in a shooting position. This measurement did not include the length of the pile. In northwestern Alaska, however, the distance was measured from the "tip of the extended left thumb to the inner end of the right collar bone, but if the man happened to be short-armed he usually measured from the tip of the left forefinger instead of from the thumb" (Nelson, 1899:155). These measurements may have been altered to also take into consideration the strength of the bow and the archer, as was done among the Copper Eskimos (Stefansson, 1914:89-90).

Murdoch found that near Point Barrow he was able to purchase only a few three-feathered arrows, and that most arrows had two feathers that had been split in half and attached to the shaft at right angles. Most of the arrows in the Beechey and Belcher collections (fig. 7, Catalogue Numbers 16-23) have two feathers lashed to the shaft in parallel planes. This arrangement is similar to the vanes attached to the butt of an East Greenland throwing harpoon (Thalbitzer, 1914:415, fig. 113). Both types of fletching are illustrated by Nelson (1899:plate 61).

Murdoch (1892:201) mentioned that the fore end of the feather was "almost always twisted about one turn, evidently to make the arrow revolve in flight, like a rifle ball". This feature is not noted in the specimens in the Beechey and Belcher collections; indeed, it seems that the two designs differ fundamentally: one is aided in accuracy by a spiraling, "rifled" motion, but the other is "cybernetically" controlled by the planar fletching. In practise, the Copper Eskimos allowed considerable latitude in the acceptable condition of the fletching; some arrows in use were far from properly fletched, having broken, missing, or twisted feathers (Stefansson, 1914:95-96).

The feathers most commonly used on arrows were the feathers of birds of prey; that is, eagles, hawks and owls, but loon or gull feathers were also used (Murdoch, 1892:201; Stefansson, 1914:95-96). The Noatak River Eskimos in historic times used goshawk (*Accipiter gentilis*) feathers (Hall, 1969:77). The Copper Eskimos considered ptarmigan (*Lagopus mutus*) feathers to be poor (Stefansson, 1914:95-96).

Three types of arrows, each serving a different function, are represented in the Beechey and Belcher collections (see Fig. 7). Number 15 is similar to arrows of a type identified by Murdoch (1892:202-203) as intended primarily for use against bears, and it resembles one illustrated by him (1892:203, fig. 186*a*). Murdoch points to the useful feature of combining the chert cutting edge with an antler barb to hold the pile in the wound. An arrow of this type was illustrated by Beechey in his hydrographic sketches (Plate V).

Numbers 16-19 and 21 were probably intended for caribou, judging from the barb and cross section of the pile. Murdoch states that the piles of caribou arrows were left loose in the shaft so that the pile would be retained in the wound and not be pulled out by the shaft. He was told that a caribou wounded this way would "sleep once and die" (Murdoch, 1892:205). Stefansson considered hunting with a bow and arrow to be more efficient than hunting with a rifle because once an animal was struck by an arrow the pain of the wound would cause it to lie down quickly (Stefansson, 1914:96). Numbers 20 and 22 differ slightly from the caribou arrows in that the piles are made of ivory, but in other respects they fit Murdoch's description. Arrows with a type of pile closely resembling that of number 20 were sketched by Choris at Kotzebue Sound in 1816 (Choris, 1822:plate 1) (Plate I).

Number 23 is possibly a fish arrow because of its two pronged head. A similar specimen is known from Nunivak Island (Nelson, 1899:160, fig. 44, 7). This type is well known from the lower Yukon area and farther south in Alaska, where fish are more plentiful than in the north. Its presence in Belcher's collection is puzzling: perhaps he purchased it from Eskimos who had previously made a trade for it or, what is more likely, perhaps he purchased it from the Pacific Eskimos when he visited them in command of H.M.S. *Sulphur* and it was subsequently mislabelled. It should be noted, however, that in the early 1880s Jacobsen collected a similar two-pronged arrow, possibly at Norton Sound, and recorded that it was used for bird hunting (Woldt, 1884:151, fig. 19).

The practice of putting ownership marks on objects—such as those on numbers 16 and 19—was widespread in northwestern Alaska (Boas, 1899:217). Choris in 1816 noticed ownership marks on arrows used by the Kotzebue Sound Eskimos and he was the first observer to call attention to them, correctly identifying their purpose:

> Ces signes ne se répètent point sur les effets d'un autre; il nous a semblé que c'etait dans le même but qu'aux îles Aléoutiennes, et dans l'île Kadiak, où les habitants marquent les flèches dont ils se servent pour la chasse de la baleine, ou de quelque autre animal, d'un signe particulier; ce qui, d'après une convention établie dès long-temps, assure la possession de l'animal blessé, en quelque lieu qu'il se trouve, au propriétaire de ces armes. Nous avons vu de ces flèches marquées ainsi chez les habitants du golfe de Kotzebue (Choris, 1822:11).

Descriptions of the nine arrows collected by Beechey and Belcher follow.

15. Beechey Collection, no. A.M. 739
    Length, 77.1 cm.; diameter of shaft, 9.5 mm.; weight, 33.6 gm. (Fig. 7:15)

This specimen has lost its chert point. The socket hole has a depth of 13 mm., and there is a lashing of three-strand caribou sinew twine around the mouth of the socket hole. The pile is made of caribou antler and is 17.2 cm. long, including the basal tang, which is 2.2 cm. The tang, which was inserted into the socket hole of the arrow shaft, has two small knobs to aid in retaining the pile in the shaft. The pile is oval in cross section. The shaft is made of spruce and is round in cross section except near the nock where it is oval. The nock has a 3 mm. diameter groove for the insertion of the bowstring; the groove runs at a right angle to the long axis of the cross section ovals of both the pile and the shaft. The fletching is composed of three pieces; each is about 14 cm. long and is a portion of a feather halved along its central quill. Both ends of the pieces are lashed to the shaft with unbraided sinew.

There are eleven arrow points, similar to the type which would have been used in this specimen, in the British Museum's Belcher Collection (B.M. Nos. 8250-60, p. 102).

16. Beechey Collection, Museum no. A.M. 737
    Length, 77.5 cm.; diameter of shaft, 9.0 mm.; weight, 34.0 gm. (Fig. 7:16)

This arrow has an antler five-barbed pile with an ownership mark (⟍). The pile is triangular in cross section and, including its basal tang, is 19.0 cm. long. The fletching is composed of two trimmed feathers attached to the shaft in parallel planes, unlike the arrangement of number 15. The feathers are lashed to the shaft near the nock with unbraided sinew, but at the fore end they have only been inserted into a slit in the shaft. The nock groove is 3 mm. in diameter and is parallel to the long axis of the cross section of the pile. The groove is perpendicular to the plane of the fletching. The shaft is spruce, round for most of its length, but oval near the nock.

17. Belcher Collection, Museum no. P.R. 681
    Length, 80.5 cm.; diameter of shaft, 10 mm.; weight, 36.7 gm. (Fig. 7:17)

The visible portion of the pile of this arrow is 20.2 cm. long. The pile has three barbs, is made of antler, and is triangular in cross section. The spruce shaft is round for most of its length but tapers to an oval near the nock. The fletching is about 18 cm. long and is attached in the same manner as number 16. At one time there may have been a lashing at the fore end of the fletching. The groove of the nock is 3.5 mm. in diameter and is perpendicular to the plane of the fletching but parallel to the long axis of the cross section of the pile.

18. Belcher Collection, Museum no. P.R. 681
    Length, 76.2 cm.; diameter of shaft, 10 mm.; weight, 39.6 gm. (Fig. 7:18)

This is a very crude specimen, having the appearance of hasty construction. The pile is made of antler, and the visible part is 19.6 cm. long. It has two fully formed barbs as well as two rudimentary ones. Its cross section is triangular. The shaft is spruce and has a lashing of unbraided sinew around the socket hole. The arrow is fletched and lashed in a manner similar to number 16. The nock groove is 4 mm. in diameter; it is perpendicular to the plane of the fletching and parallel to the long axis of the cross section of the pile.

19. Belcher Collection, unnumbered.
    Length, 73.8 cm.; diameter of shaft, 10 mm.; weight, 36.0 gm.; according to Pitt Rivers
    Museum Catalogue, collected at Icy Cape. (Fig. 7:19)

The antler pile of this arrow contains an ownership mark (⟋). The visible portion of the pile is 14.8 cm. long; it has one large, crude barb and is triangular in cross section. The shaft is spruce and is lashed at the socket with unbraided sinew. The fletching is about 14 cm. in length and is similar to that of number 16, with similar lashing and fastening. The diameter of the nock groove is 3 mm.

20. Belcher Collection, unnumbered.
Length, 69.3 cm.; diameter of shaft, 10 mm.; weight, 28.1 gm. (Fig. 7:20)

The pile of this arrow is made of walrus ivory with one large barb, and its visible length is 10.8 cm. It is triangular in cross section. The spruce shaft has a lashing of unbraided sinew at the socket. The lashing and fletching are similar to the lashing and fletching of number 16. The nock groove is 3 mm. in diameter; it is perpendicular to the plane of the fletching and parallel to the plane of the barb.

21. Belcher Collection, Museum no. P.R. 1292
Length, 76.2 cm.; diameter of shaft, 11 mm.; weight, 32.5 gm. (Fig. 7:21)

This specimen is similar to number 19, even to the ownership mark. Its antler pile is 14.1 cm. in length, including the basal tang, which is 2 cm. long. The conical tang has two knobs, on opposite sides, to improve retention of the pile in the shaft socket. In cross section the pile is triangular. The fletching is 20 cm. long, but in other respects this arrow is identical with those for that of number 19.

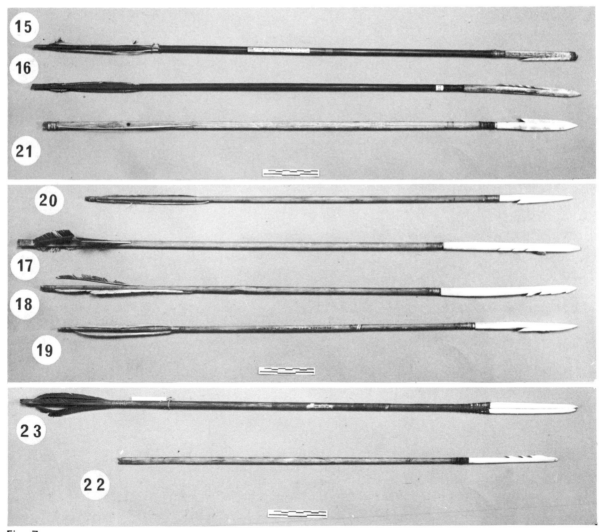

Fig. 7

22. Belcher Collection, Museum no. P.R. 681
    Length, 59.5 cm.; diameter of shaft, 8 mm.; weight, 19.6 gm. (Fig. 7:22)

This arrow is very crudely made and, judging from its shortness, may have been a boy's practise arrow. The pile, made of ivory, has seven rudimentary barbs. Its visible length is 12.3 cm., and it is triangular in cross section. The fletching has been destroyed, but traces of the lashing and insertion slits reveal that it was approximately 12 cm. long and that it was similar to the fletching of number 16. The diameter of the nock groove is 3 mm.; it is perpendicular to the plane of the fletching and parallel to the long axis of the cross section of the pile. This arrow has a spruce shaft.

23. Belcher Collection, Museum no. P.R. 860
    Length, 73.8 cm.; diameter of shaft, 9 mm.; weight, 38.6 gm.; according to Pitt Rivers Museum Catalogue, collected at Icy Cape. (Fig. 7:23)

The pile of this arrow is made of two parallel ivory rods tightly lashed together and affixed to the spruce shaft by three-strand sinew twine. Each rod is approximately 15.3 cm. in length. The shaft is 60.4 cm. long, round, and tapers to an oval near the nock. The fletching is composed of three feathers, split longitudinally as in number 15. Two of the feathers are lashed on one side of the shaft, projecting at angles from the top and bottom of the oval; the other projects perpendicularly from the shaft, directly opposite the nock groove. The nock groove has been cut parallel to the long axis of the pile.

Arrow shaft straightener

Belcher described the use of the shaft straightener in arrow manufacture thus:
> The arrows . . . are . . . not made as one would imagine from the straightest-grained timber that could be met with, but from that which happens to be present on the beach. They are straightened instead of bent by steam in the manner following. Having shaved the shaft to nearly the thickness required, it is then bound round with the finest shavings in a spiral direction. It is then immersed in water and held over a fire of live coals, wetting it repeatedly with water until they deem it sufficiently steamed. Held by one end it is apparent from the spiral mode of binding, that it may be instantly slipped through and disencumbered of its covering. It is then treated with the . . . [shaft straightener], and readily brought into its required straightness (Belcher, 1861:142).

24. Belcher Collection, Museum no. 1969.34.10
    Length, 14.5 cm. (Fig. 8)

Arrow shaft straighteners are well represented in ethnographic collections from Alaska. Though not called arrow shaft straighteners, similar items—with carvings of animal heads—were illustrated from the Diomede Islands and Cape Nome by Nelson (1899:plate 40, *2,3*) and from

Sledge Island by Hoffman (1897:plate 7, *3*). Beechey also sketched one of these (Plate V). Farther to the east, among the Copper Eskimos of Coronation Gulf and Victoria Island, these items seem to have been made with less care and ornamentation (Stefansson, 1914:95, fig. 40). The piece in the Belcher collection, made of mammoth ivory, is especially handsome.

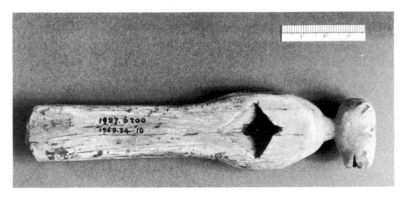

Fig. 8

Mammoth ivory is found at several places along the coast of northwestern Alaska in Pleistocene muck beds. It can be quarried at Eschscholtz Bay—where Beechey collected the bones of several extinct animals—and near Wainwright Inlet (Bailey and Hendee, 1926:28).

The British Museum's Belcher Collection also contains an arrow shaft straightener from Point Hope (B.M. No. 8228, p. 101).

Arrow Fletching Implements

Arrow fletching implements (feather setters) were used to fasten the fletching to the shaft of an arrow by forcing the feather's quill into the shaft. They were made in a variety of forms and were among the collections made at Point Barrow by Murdoch (1892:291-94).

25. Belcher Collection, unnumbered.
Length, 15.9 cm.; walrus ivory. (Fig. 9:25)

26. Beechey Collection, Museum no. A.M. 771
Length, 13.6 cm.; walrus ivory. (Fig. 9:26)

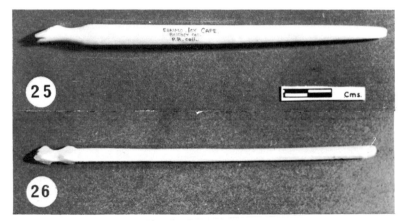

Fig. 9

The feather setters collected by Belcher and Beechey are distinguished by their narrow, spatulate tips which allow ease of penetration into the grain of the wood. Neither specimen bears a central hole for suspension on a line with other archery implements carried in a hunter's tool kit.

Harpoons

Because they were so efficient and well designed, harpoons are among the most admired items of Eskimo material culture. The most important feature of the Eskimo harpoon is its toggling head. When the head becomes detached from the harpoon shaft after striking an animal, it is designed to turn within the wound at a ninety-degree angle to the force on the harpoon line and thus render itself far more resistant to extraction by an animal's thrashing. The toggling motion occurs because of a basal spur on the head which causes the rotation.

The force on the harpoon line that causes the head to toggle and then to tire the quarry is provided either by the hunter himself when smaller game is being sought or by an inflated float, or floats, when walruses and whales are being hunted.

Harpoons may be divided into two formal classes: those with and those without fixed foreshafts. Fixed foreshaft harpoons were designed to enable the hunter to thrust the harpoon head deeply into the quarry's body from close range. This class includes whaling harpoons and harpoons designed for capturing seals at their breathing holes. Harpoons with moveable foreshafts were, on the other hand, intended primarily to be thrown. The moveable foreshaft allowed the harpoon shaft to become disengaged from its toggling head immediately on striking the quarry. This feature insured both that the head would not be forced out of the wound by the torque from the moving harpoon shaft and that the proper functioning of the toggling head would not be impeded.

Both classes of harpoons may be subdivided into those with and without ice picks. A harpoon with an ice pick at the butt assisted the hunter in travelling over the ice and in testing its thickness. It could also be used to administer the *coup de grace* to the quarry. Harpoons without ice picks were intended to be used from boats.

The British Museum has, in its Beechey Collection, two harpoons (nos. 28/12-13/34 and 28/12-13/35) that are nearly identical with each other and in general resemble the Beechey and Belcher harpoons at the Pitt Rivers Museum (Figs. 10-15). An interesting difference is that the British Museum implements have a rectantular slot in the socket piece for the reception of the foreshaft while the Pitt Rivers Museum harpoons have conical slots. One of the British Museum specimens is labelled "St. Lawrence Ids".

Each of the Pitt Rivers harpoons has, or at one time had, a retaining line attached both to the ice pick and to the socket piece, which was also fastened to the shaft at one or more places. If either of these pieces became detached from the shaft during use, the retaining line would have prevented its loss. The foreshaft also would have been retained because of its attachment to the socket piece. The retaining line no doubt saved the hunter the work of making new pieces and allowed repairs to be made in the field.

Descriptions of Beechey's and Belcher's harpoons at the Pitt Rivers Museum follow.

27. Beechey Collection, Museum no. A.M. 676
    Length, 239 cm.; weight, 2160 gm. According to Pitt Rivers Museum Catalogue, collected at Kotzebue Sound. (Fig. 10, A and B)

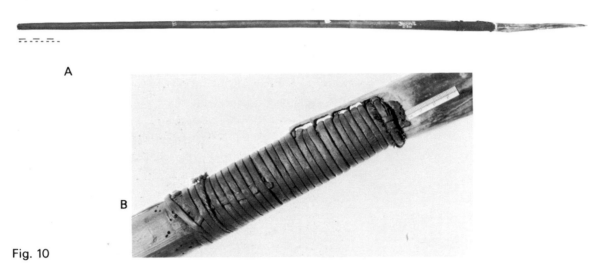

A

B

Fig. 10

The foreshaft of this harpoon is of walrus ivory and is approximately 50.8 cm. long. It is tightly affixed to the shaft and the lashing allows it no movement. The lashing is a baleen strip strung through a series of drilled, oblong holes at the proximal end of the fore shaft. A retaining line of bearded seal (*Erignathus barbatus*) skin is pegged to the shaft 43 cm. from the foreshaft. This line would retain the foreshaft, should it be broken from the shaft during use. The shaft, of unpainted spruce, is roughly conical and tapers from about 44 mm. to about 26 mm. in diameter.

This specimen is listed in the catalogue as a harpoon, but the labelling is confusing. Because of its length, weight and fixed foreshaft, it may have been a bowhead whale (*Baleana mysticetus*) harpoon; but it is not closely similar to whale harpoons from northern or western Alaska. Hence it is possible that it could have come from St. Lawrence Island. However, if the museum catalogue's record of provenance is correct, and this specimen *was* collected in Kotzebue Sound, then it may have been intended for use not as a harpoon, but as an ice chisel to cut holes through sea and river ice for hook-and-line fishing or for the setting of nets.

28. Belcher Collection, Museum no. P.R. 871
    Length, 213 cm.; weight, 954 gm. According to Pitt Rivers Museum Catalogue, collected at Icy Cape. (Fig. 11, A and B)

This fine specimen unfortunately lacks the foreshaft and head assembly. The socket piece, carved from walrus ivory, was made to resemble a bear's head. The bear's mouth encloses the socket hole, which is conical, 11 mm. wide and 11 mm. deep. The socket hole allowed the proximal end of the foreshaft to move somewhat and thus to detach itself under pressure. The socket piece is 22.4 cm. long and is lashed to the shaft at the base with a baleen strip 8mm. wide. Near the base of the socket piece's tang there are two drilled holes (5 mm. in diameter) through which runs a sealskin retaining line. The spruce shaft is nearly perfectly cylindrical and about 2.8 cm. in diameter. It has a small ivory knob approximately 82 cm. from the front end of the socket piece. This probably served to maintain the tension on the harpoon line and kept the harpoon head in the proper position during throwing or thrusting. There are remnants of a lashing for a finger rest 101 cm. from the front end of the socket piece. The lashing is three-strand sinew twine, about 1 mm. in diameter. The ice pick is a beautifully formed piece of walrus ivory, 48.6 cm. long. It is lashed to the butt of the shaft with three-strand sinew twine as well as with a baleen strip about 11 mm. wide. Fragments of a sealskin retaining line also remain.

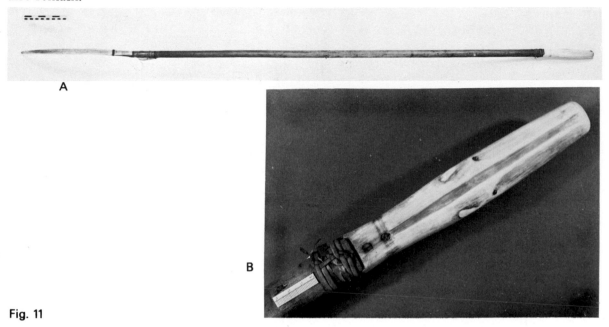

Fig. 11

29. Belcher Collection, Museum no. P.R. 868
    Length, 191 cm.; weight, 634.5 gm. According to Pitt Rivers Museum Catalogue, collected at Icy Cape and "used for spearing fish". (Fig. 12, A and B)

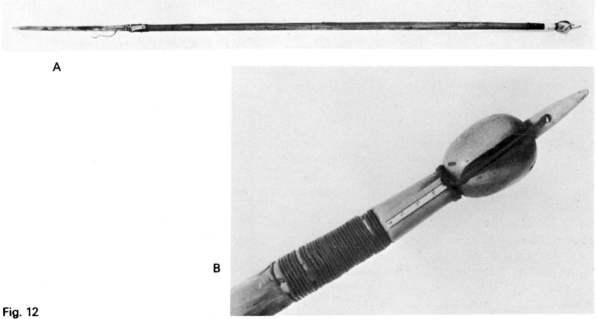

Fig. 12

This harpoon lacks its head assembly. The socket piece and foreshaft are of unusual shapes: the foreshaft is only 4.3 cm. long, and the antler socket piece has a large bulbar protruberance at the distal end. It is lashed to the shaft with three-strand sinew twine. The shaft is very light and of spruce, about 2.5 cm. in diameter. The ice pick is handsomely made of ivory, 44.3 cm. long. It has a drilled hole in the basal tang, probably for the retaining line, which has been lost.

Belcher sketched a similar model in his journal (Plate VI); he noted that it was used for taking marine mammals. His rendering of the harpoon head is probably incorrect, however. More likely the plane of the blade was parallel to the line hole, not perpendicular to it, as he has depicted it. Harpoon heads with a perpendicular blade are rare in later Western Eskimo seal and walrus harpoons. On the other hand, most whaling harpoon heads possess this feature.

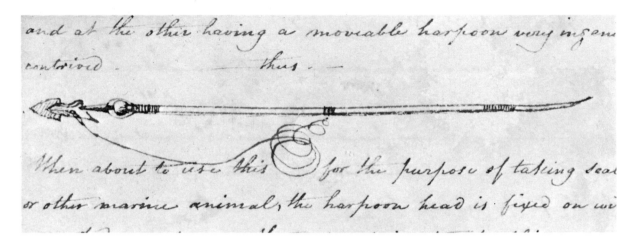

Plate VI Belcher's sketch of a harpoon from his Journal. Courtesy of the University of British Columbia Library.

30. Beechey Collection, Museum no. A.M. 682
     Length, 206 cm.; weight, 128 gm. According to the 1836 Ashmolean Museum Catalogue, collected at Kotzebue Sound. (Fig. 13, A-I)

This fine specimen has an ivory foreshaft 26 cm. long, which is lashed to the socket piece by a sealskin line that runs through a hole drilled near the middle of the foreshaft. The socket piece is also ivory and is fixed to the shaft with seven alternating bands of black and white baleen strips. The socket piece is secured by the same retaining line that runs the length of the shaft and secures the ice pick. The shaft is unpainted spruce, about 3.8 cm. in diameter. A groove runs the length of the shaft to hold the retaining line, thus minimizing wear on this important lashing. About 75 cm. from the tip of the foreshaft the retaining line is seized to the shaft with a strip of baleen, and both ends of the strip are inserted into slits in the harpoon shaft. A finger rest of ivory is carved to represent a seal's head and is lashed to the shaft with baleen strips 94.5 cm. from the tip of the foreshaft. The carefully made ivory ice pick is 43 cm. long and is lashed with the end of the retaining line, which, after being led down the shaft and through two small holes on the ice pick, is wrapped twelve times around the base of the shaft.

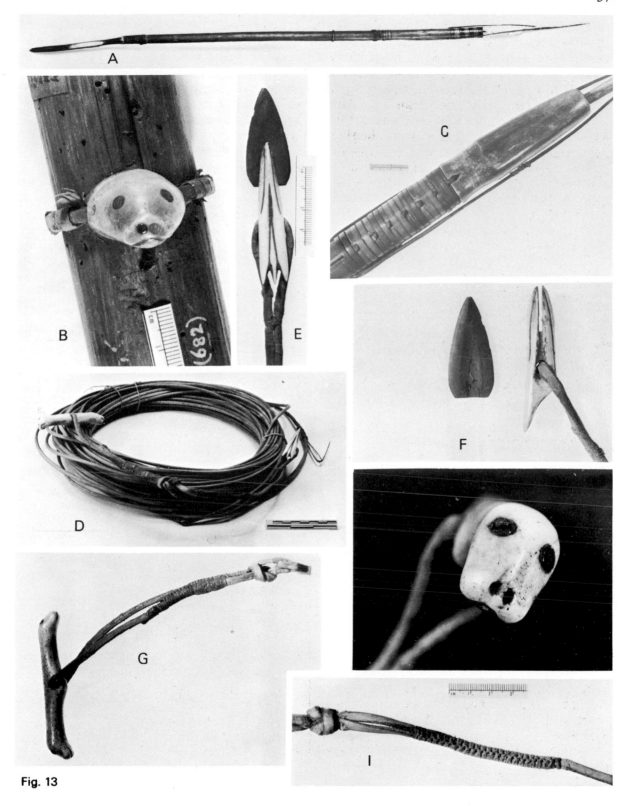

Fig. 13

The harpoon head assembly consists of toggle, line, head and blade. The harpoon line is forty metres long and has a toggle at the base for retention in the hand. The line is made from bearded seal skin, and at both ends it is seized to itself to form loops that attach the head and toggle. The toggle is ivory, with each end carved to represent a seal's head; and inset eyes are blue glass beads. The harpoon head is made of ivory, and it has one spur that is separated into three barbs. The blade is slate and its plane is parallel to that of the line hole. The line has a small baleen loop attached to it 38 cm. from the head. The loop could have been fastened over a small peg on the shaft to maintain tension on the line and keep the head and foreshaft in the proper position during throwing or thrusting.

Specimen number 30 is representative of a well-known type of harpoon in western Alaska. Mason illustrated one from the Bering Sea area and Boas mentioned one from "Alaska" (Mason, 1902:199, plate 10; Boas, 1888:472, fig. 390).

31. Beechey Collection, Museum no. A.M. 683
    Length, 167 cm.; weight, 129 gm. According to Pitt Rivers Museum Catalogue, collected at Kotzebue Sound. (Fig. 14, A and B)

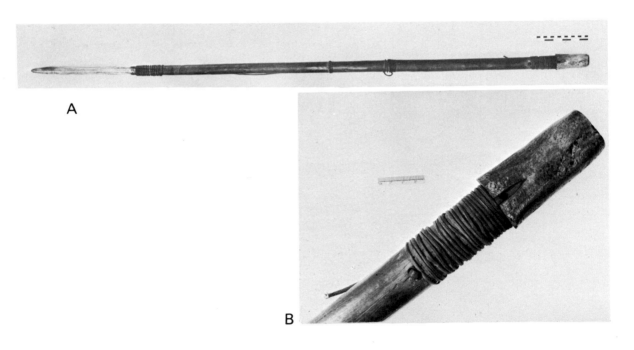

A

B

Fig. 14

This specimen lacks a foreshaft and harpoon head assembly. The socket piece is made of either walrus baculum or mandible and it is lashed to the shaft with a line of bearded seal skin. The shaft is spruce, about 3.5 cm. in diameter. The 37.5 cm. ice pick is ivory and very well made. A retaining line runs the length of the shaft and connects the socket piece and ice pick. It is seized to the shaft by the finger rest lashings and another lashing closer to the socket piece. The harpoon line could be secured by looping it through this second lashing and thus maintaining tension on the harpoon head and foreshaft. The finger rest is ivory and is lashed to the shaft with a sealskin line.

Bladder harpoon

Bladder harpoons differ from other types of harpoon in that an inflated bladder, intestine or stomach is attached to the shaft. These harpoons were designed to be towed behind an animal after it had been struck because the drag created by the shaft and bladder impeded its progress, causing it to tire quickly.

32. Belcher Collection, Museum no. P.R. 881
    Length, 230 cm.; weight, 645.2 gm. According to Pitt Rivers Museum Catalogue, collected from the "Western Eskimo". (Fig. 15, A-E)

Belcher's superb specimen of a bladder harpoon probably was incorrectly labelled by him and was not collected in northwestern Alaska. Similar types are not described in the ethnographical literature for that area, and the closest resemblances are found far to the south of Bering Strait. Mason illustrated three similar bladder harpoons, one from Bristol Bay and two from the Kuskokwim River, and Birket-Smith showed one from the Kodiak Island Eskimos of the North Pacific (Mason: 1902:288-89, 297; Birket-Smith, 1941:135, fig. 13). Belcher probably obtained this specimen either when he visited Prince William Sound in 1837 or when he stopped at Kodiak Island in 1839 (Belcher, 1843).

The head of Belcher's harpoon is bone, and it has a grey chert blade that lashed into the socket with a two-strand sinew line. A spruce sheath on the head is attached to the shaft by a fine two-strand line. The foreshaft is also of bone and is seized to the line that runs from the harpoon head to the bladder. The line is apparently covered with a lightly sewn strip of intestine, presumably for waterproofness. The line between the head and the bladder is sinew woven into an eight-strand sennit (Ashley, 1944:493). The bladder is made of the stomach or intestine of, possibly, a walrus, and it is lashed to the shaft at both ends with a three-strand sinew line. The inflation nozzle of the bladder is bone.

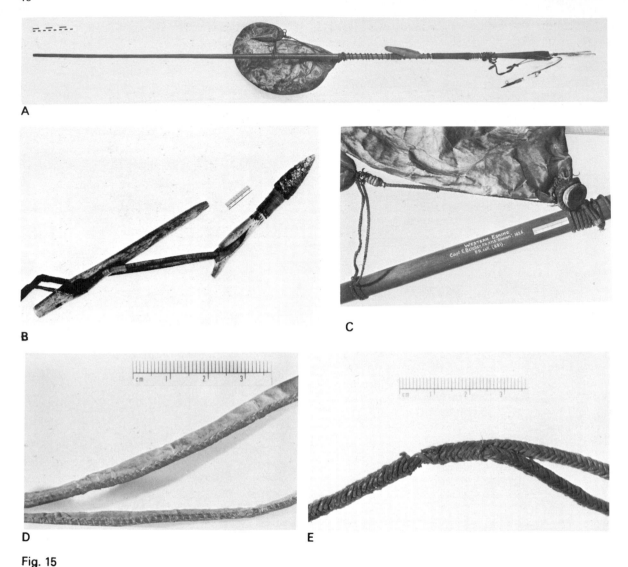

A

B

C

D

E

Fig. 15

Harpoon foreshafts

From the shape of the two foreshafts collected by Beechey, it seems probable that they originated in the eastern Arctic rather than in Alaska. The most likely explanation for the incorrect record of provenance is that when the Beechey collection was stored at the Ashmolean Museum along with artefacts from Parry's second voyage to the Arctic, some items were mislabelled.

33. Beechey Collection, Museum no. A.M. 684b.
    Length, 42.6 cm. According to the 1836 Ashmolean Museum Catalogue, collected at Point Franklin. (Fig. 16:33)

Specimen number 33 is probably incorrectly labelled. It is heavier than other types noted from north Alaska, and it is made from two pieces of ivory lashed together, which was unusual in that area. It closely resembles a Central Eskimo type collected by Boas on Baffin Island in the 1880s (Boas, 1888:494, fig. 429).

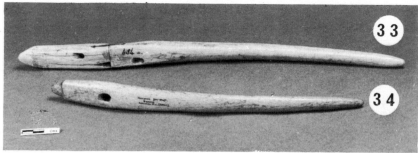

Fig. 16

34. Beechey Collection, Museum no. A.M. 684c.
Length, 31.9 cm. According to the 1836 Ashmolean Museum Catalogue, possibly collected at Point Franklin. (Fig. 16:34)

In general shape and in the arrangement of the holes for the retaining lines this foreshaft resembles number 33. It is made from a single piece of whalebone.

Bladder dart

Darts differ from harpoons in the functioning of the head. A harpoon head is usually designed to "toggle" in a wound, an action that requires a large basal spur and great force to drive the head deeply. A dart head, on the other hand, is designed not to "toggle"; instead of a spur it has a number of lateral barbs with which to hold itself in a wound. A dart, thus, does not require a heavy shaft to ensure a deeply seated head, but its dragging power, even with a bladder attachment, cannot be as great as that of a harpoon. Its use is restricted to smaller game.

Bladder darts were in use in Hudson Bay in the late nineteenth century (Boas, 1901:78-80) and are still used by the Igloolik Eskimos of northeastern Canada (Crowe, 1969:70-72). Small inflation nozzles have been found in archaeological sites near Point Barrow (Ford, 1959: 114-15), but when Murdoch (1892:215) lived there from 1881 to 1883 bladder darts were no longer in use. At that time only seal darts, without a bladder, were being used. Before the beginning of this century the Eskimos of that area continued to be able to make complicated sennits using as many as sixteen strands (Brower, 1899:597), but there is no evidence that these lines were used in conjunction with a bladder dart.

The use of bladder darts persisted somewhat longer in the south near Norton Sound. Nelson's collection contained one (Nelson, 1899:189, plate 55); and Edmonds obtained one there in the 1890s (Edmonds, 1966:123-24). In that area rifles were not as readily obtainable as in the north and hence the bladder dart continued to be a useful weapon for seal hunting.

35. Belcher Collection, Museum no. P.R. 875
Length, 153 cm.; weight, 223 gm. According to Pitt Rivers Museum Catalogue, collected at "Behring Straits". (Fig. 17: A-G)

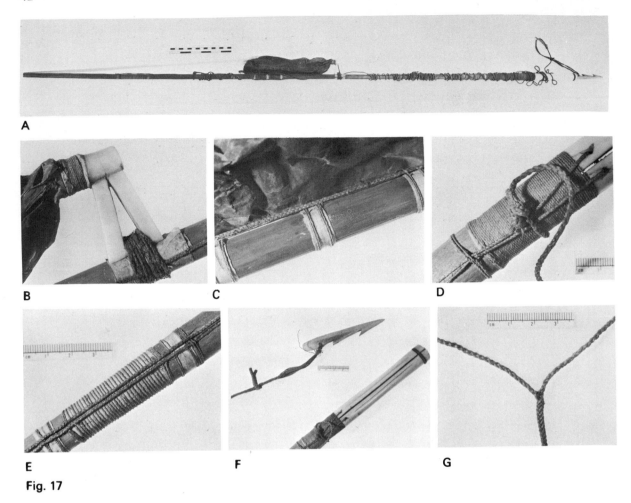

Fig. 17

This bladder dart, like the bladder harpoon in Figure 15, was probably collected from the Pacific Eskimos by Belcher when he was in command of H.M.S. *Sulphur*. The exceptionally fine workmanship is uncharacteristic of implements from northwestern Alaska. A nearly identical bladder dart from Kodiak Island was illustrated by Mason (1902:plate 19); like number 32, it has eight-strand sennit weaving in its larger lines.

Darts

Darts of the type collected by Beechey were still common in the 1880s in northern Alaska (Mason, 1902: plate 11; Murdoch, 1892: 215, fig. 203). They were usually propelled with the aid of a throwing stick such as shown in figure 20 and were used from a kayak to take small seals. The dart was designed so that the shaft would act as a drogue. Once the quarry had been struck, the shaft would disengage from the head, and, if on a Y-shaped line, the shaft would be towed at right angles, increasing the drag (Murdoch, 1892:215-16).

The British Museum possesses two of Beechey's darts (nos. 28/12-13/31 and 28/12-13/32), and, like the specimens in the Pitt Rivers collections, their crudity and apparently hasty manufacture stand in contrast to the careful workmanship noted in harpoons.

36. Beechey Collection, Museum no. A.M. 717
    Length, 188.5 cm.; weight, 59 gm. According to the 1836 Ashmolean Museum Catalogue, collected at Cape Thompson. (Fig. 18:36)

The dart shown at the top of figure 18 was crudely made. Its roughness suggests that it may have been very quickly manufactured near the hunting area. The head is made of bone and has three barbs on one side and two on the other. It is 7.5 cm. long and has a wedge-shaped, tapering tang. The line hole is drilled and has a diameter of 3 mm. The socket piece is made of roughly shaped ivory which has no holes for a retaining line; the hole for the socket is lined with wood. The shaft is spruce, also roughly shaped; it tapers in diameter from about 32 mm. at the socket piece to about 9 mm. at the butt. The line on this dart is sealskin, about 3.5 mm. thick. It runs from the head to the shaft where it is fastened by a clove hitch; the free end is inserted in a slit in the shaft. Unlike many darts wherein the head is joined to the shaft by a Y-formed line, this specimen has only a single line.

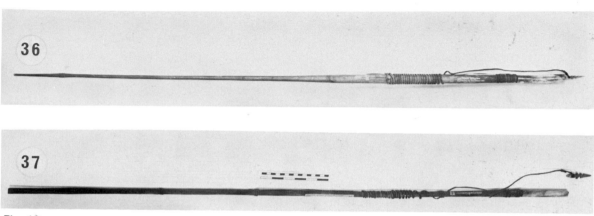

Fig. 18

37. Beechey Collection, Museum no. A.M. 719
    Length, 133.5 cm.; weight, 127 gm. According to Pitt Rivers Museum Catalogue, collected at Kotzebue Sound. (Fig. 18:37)

Like number 36, this dart is crudely made. The head is of bone, 7.0 cm. long; it has a tapering, wedge-shaped tang and a gouged and drilled line hole. There are three barbs on one side and two on the other. The socket piece is made from ivory, and the socket hole is lined with wood. The spruce shaft tapers in diameter from about 18 mm. at the socket piece to about 12 mm. at the butt. A broken retaining line of three-strand sinew is attached through a hole near the tang on the socket piece. The line was used as the lashing for the junction of the socket piece and the shaft, and it then led about 83 cm. along the shaft, where it was tied. The line attaching the dart head to the shaft is sealskin, about 3 mm. wide. It forms a Y and is attached to the shaft at two points.

Bird spear

Bird spears are known to have been made in a wide range of forms, all of which included the feature of three splayed prongs lashed equidistantly around the circumference of a shaft. The prongs, whether placed near the middle of the shaft or at the fore end, functioned to impale the birds or to catch their wings. Beechey sketched one with the prongs near the middle of the shaft (Plate V). The spears were generally thrown from a kayak, with the aid of a spear thrower (Fig. 20) at sitting water fowl. A spear similar to the one Beechey collected at Point Franklin (Fig. 19) was illustrated by Nelson (1899:plate 59, *3*) from St. Michael, and Belcher (n.d.:65) mentioned seeing one near Kotzebue Sound. This type, with the prongs attached at the fore end, does not appear in Murdoch's (1892) ethnography and hence may not have been used at Point Barrow in the 1880s.

Nelson (1899:151-52) mentioned that bird spears were about four feet long and that they could be thrown overhand to strike the birds from above or, should the birds be wary, could be thrown "side arm" to skim along the surface of the water. Flying birds would have been taken with bolas (Figs. 24-27).

38. Beechey Collection, Museum no. A.M. 724
     Length, 25.8 cm. According to the 1836 Ashmolean Museum Catalogue, collected at Point Franklin. (Fig. 19)

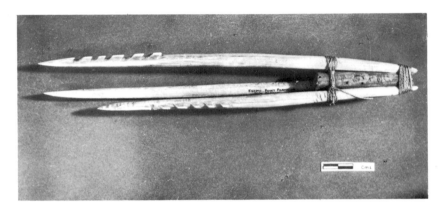

Fig. 19

The bird spear is damaged and only the extreme fore-end of the spear remains. The three prongs are ivory, each approximately 25.5 cm. long. Two of the prongs have six barbs near the front tip and one has nine; the barbs project on the outer edge of the prongs. The prongs are lashed to the spruce shaft with three-strand sinew twine, about 0.8 mm. thick. The shaft is broken near the base of the prongs.

Spear-throwers

Spear-throwers, by functionally increasing the user's forearm, allowed bird spears and darts to be thrown with greater speed. Nelson (1899:153) reported that among Eskimos near Unalakleet the length of a spear thrower was equal to the distance between the tip of the right elbow and the extended index finger of the user.

Beechey described the use of a spear thrower by a Buckland River Eskimo in Eschscholtz Bay:

> We met several native caiacs, and had an exhibition of the skill of one of the Esquimaux in throwing his dart, which he placed in a slip, a small wooden instrument about a foot in length, with a hole cut in the end to receive the forefinger, and a notch for the thumb. The stick being thus grasped, the dart was laid along a groove in the slip, and embraced by the middle finger and the thumb. The man next propelled his caiac with speed in order to communicate greater velocity to the dart, and then whirled it through

the air to a considerable distance. As there was no mark, we could not judge of his skill in taking aim (Beechey, 1831:I, 324).

Belcher's curiosity led him also to comment on the dart and spear thrower—apparently to the detriment of his ethnographic collection:

> Another smaller spear with small moveable head is likewise made use of for throwing at objects 15 to 20 yards distant they taper at the opposite end and seldom exceed 5 feet. From frequent trial I found they went with considerable force penetrating 1 inch into a water cask at 15 yds. These are thrown by the assistance of a stock 18 inches long in the end of which the small end of the spear is inserted . . . and increases the force considerably. Great art however is required to use it properly (Belcher, n.d.:65).

Three spear throwers at the Pitt Rivers Museum were collected by Belcher and Beechey.

39. Beechey Collection, Museum no. A.M. 722
    Length, 41.2 cm.; weight, 77 gm. According to Pitt Rivers Museum Catalogue, collected at Kotzebue Sound. (Fig. 20:39)

Spear-thrower number 39 is made of spruce; it has an ivory tang at the tip which is mortised and lashed into the spruce frame. The tang is for insertion in a groove in the butt of the spear. It is intended for a right-handed person.

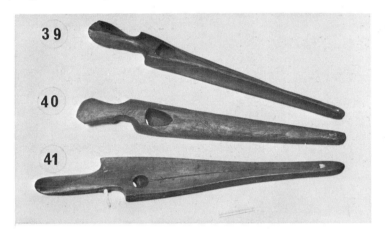

Fig. 20

40. Beechey Collection, Museum no. A.M. 721.
    Length, 42.5 cm.; weight, 100 gm. According to Pitt Rivers Museum Catalogue, collected at Kotzebue Sound. (Fig. 20:40)

Designed for a right-handed user, this spear thrower has a spruce body and an ivory tang mortised to the frame.

41. Belcher Collection, Museum no. P.R. 214
    Length, 45.2 cm.; weight, 161 gm. According to Pitt Rivers Museum Catalogue, probably collected between Icy Cape and Point Barrow. (Fig. 20:41)

Like the other two spear throwers, this one is made for a right-handed thrower. It has a spruce body with an ivory tang mortised to the frame. It also has an ivory peg for a finger rest.

Number 41 bears a label indicating that it was purchased in the eastern Arctic by Belcher when he was in command of H.M.S. *Assistance*. This voyage to Arctic Canada took place in the 1850s as part of the search for the missing expedition of Sir John Franklin. The object does not look like eastern Arctic types, but closely resembles spear-throwers made in western Alaska. Without doubt it is incorrectly labelled. The mistake in labelling, as on other pieces, may have occurred many years after Belcher's return from the Arctic when his artefacts were transferred to the Pitt Rivers collections.

Spear throwers of general similarity are recorded from areas as far apart as Prince William Sound (Bushnell, 1949:121, plate N; Birket-Smith, 1953:10) and Port Clarence (Nordenskiöld, 1882:571). It must be noted, though, that the British Museum's Beechey collection contains a spear-thrower (no. 28/12-13/27) that is, in general, similar to Belcher's.

Lances

The lances represented in the Beechey and Belcher collections were probably intended to be used from a kayak to spear swimming caribou. This type of lance, with a fixed head, was common from Norton Sound northward (Murdoch, 1892:242-44; Nelson, 1899:145-46). According to Murdoch, this type of lance is distinguishable from bear and whale lances because its points are not as large or as spatulate. A lance in the British Museum's Beechey collection (no. 28/12-15/27), like these specimens, is crudely finished; this suggests that lances were often made hastily near the scene of a hunt.

42. Beechey Collections, Museum no. A.M. 726
    Length, 195.7 cm.; weight, 299.5 gm. According to Pitt Rivers Museum Catalogue, collected at Kotzebue Sound. (Fig. 21, A and B)

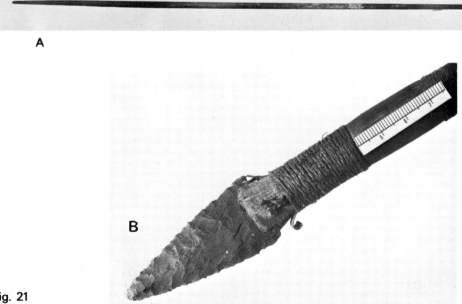

A

B

Fig. 21

Lance number 42 has a 5.8-cm.-long point of a basaltic material. The visible portion of the point is triangular and 2.5 cm. wide at the base. It is lashed to the shaft with two lengths of three-strand sinew twine. The shaft is spruce; its maximum diameter is 2.3 cm.

43. Beechey Collection, Museum no. A.M. 727
    Length, 177.0 cm.; weight 217.7 gm. According to Pitt Rivers Museum Catalogue, collected at Kotzebue Sound. (Fig. 22, A and B)

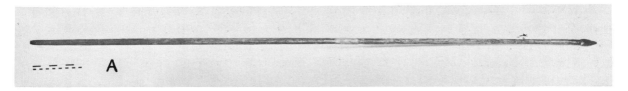

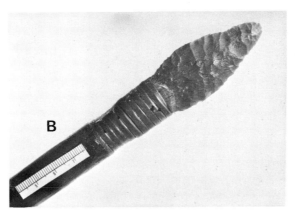

Fig. 22

The shaft of this specimen is spruce, 2.3 cm. in diameter. The point is grey chert, lashed to the shaft with light-coloured baleen; it is 7.5 cm. long and 2.9 cm. wide. The poor condition of this specimen has probably affected the weight.

44. Belcher Collection, part of Pitt Rivers Collection, unnumbered.
    Length, 204.2 cm.; weight, 367.4 gm. According to Pitt Rivers Museum Catalogue, collected at Icy Cape. (Fig. 23, A-C)

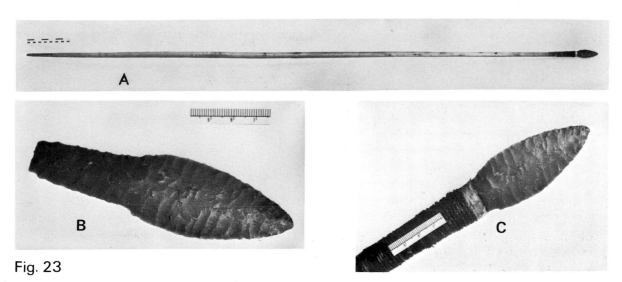

Fig. 23

This lance has a spruce shaft, 2.5 cm. in maximum diameter. Its grey chert point, which has become detached from the shaft, is 11.8 cm. long and 3.3 cm. maximum in width. The point is very skilfully flaked. There are three similar lance points in the British Museum's Belcher Collection (B.M. Nos. 8247-49). Two of them came from Cape Lisburne. A similar point was purchased by Nordenskiöld (1882:271) at Port Clarence and one was excavated from a recent burial at Point Hope (Larsen and Rainey, 1948:plate 94, 6). The fore end of the shaft was split to receive the point's base. It was then wrapped in depilated caribou skin and lashed with three-strand caribou sinew twine. Belcher gave a clear description of the flaking process used in the manufacture of the points:

> Selecting a log of wood, in which a spoon-shaped cavity was cut, they placed the splinter to be worked over it, and by pressing gently along the margin vertically, first on one side, then the other, as one would set a saw, they splintered off alternate fragments until the object, thus properly outlined, presented the spear or arrowhead form, with two cutting serrated sides. (Belcher, 1861:138-39)

The Belcher Collection at the British Museum contains a flint flaker (B.M. No. 8241) and three unfinished lance points (B.M. Nos. 8244-46), all collected at Cape Lisburne (p. 102).

Bolas

Bolas were widely used by the Eskimos of northwestern Alaska for capturing birds on the wing. The bola assemblage was carried loosely by the hunter, looped into a chain of slipknots to prevent the tangling of the lines. These loops could be quickly shaken out when the apparatus was needed. Charles Brower witnessed their use near Point Barrow in 1886, shortly before their replacement by firearms. His description follows:

> The majority used a *ka-lum-ik-toun*. This was seven small pieces of bone or ivory, the size of a man's thumb from the end of the first joint. These were attached to braided sinew, nearly three feet long. The ends of the sinew were all fastened together. Where they were joined a very small bunch of feathers was fastened, apparently to make them fly straight. The shape of the ivory was mostly round, but any other shape was also used at times. The men, and women also, used these slings. Some were experts with them, often getting two birds at one throw.
>
> In using these *ka-lum-ik-toun*, the ivory part was held in the left hand, the right hand grasping the end of the sinew. Stretching the sinew to its full length then letting go of the ivory balls, they were swung around the head once, then thrown at the flock. The ivory, spreading in all directions, coming in contact with a bird, it would wrap around the body, holding the wings and often breaking them (Brower, n.d.:240).

The use of bolas in northwestern Alaska is known to have occurred in the Birnirk culture of about A.D. 500-800 (Bockstoce, 1973:218; Ford, 1959:138-42), and their use persisted near Point Barrow until the twentieth century: Stefansson reported that in 1912 some men still used them (1914:384).

In 1940 Rainey (n.d.) was told at Point Hope that seven different shapes of bola weights had been used; among these were pear-shaped, egg-shaped, cubic, rectangular and turnip-shaped weights. He recorded that the weights of each bola were made either in a uniform shape or in seven different shapes.

Some of the bolas in the Pitt Rivers collections may have been acquired near Cape Thompson. Wolfe recorded that in August of 1826 he watched Eskimos in that area capturing birds with them (Wolfe, n.d.:119). Beechey sketched a bolas assembly in his hydrographic notes (Plate V).

45. Beechey Collection, Museum no. A.M. 666
    According to Pitt Rivers Museum Catalogue, collected from the "Western Eskimo" (Fig. 24)

This bolas has five egg-shaped bone weights, possibly of walrus baculum, averaging 16.3 gm. Each is attached to a line of three-strand caribou sinew about 50 cm. long. At their junction is a bunch of feathers (not visible in photograph) bound with three-strand sinew.

46. Beechey Collection, Museum no. A.M. 667
    According to Pitt Rivers Museum Catalogue, collected from the "Western Eskimo". (Fig. 25)

This specimen has seven pear-shaped weights averaging about 14.6 gm. They are joined together on lines of three-strand sinew about 54 cm. long. A cluster of duck feathers is fastened at their junction.

47. Beechey Collection, Museum no. A.M. 668
    According to the Pitt Rivers Museum Catalogue, collected from the "Western Eskimo". (Fig. 26)

Fig. 24 (left) and 25 (right)

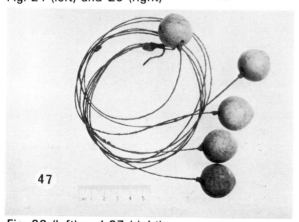
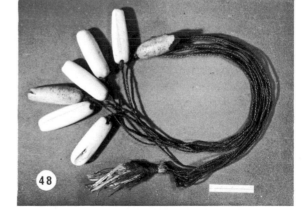

Fig. 26 (left) and 27 (right)

The five weights of this bolas average 16.5 gm. They are turnip-shaped and are probably made from walrus baculum. The lines are about 52.5 cm. long, and there are no feathers at the junction.

48. Beechey Collection, Museum no. A.M. 669
    According to the Pitt Rivers Museum Catalogue, collected from the "Western Eskimo". (Fig. 27)

The weights of this specimen are roughly cylindrical, averaging about 15.5 gm. Five are of walrus ivory and two are of bone, possibly walrus baculum. The lines are about 57 cm. long and are made from three-strand sinew. A bunch of feathers, possibly duck, are at the junction of the lines.

49. Beechey Collection, Museum no. A.M. 670
    According to the Pitt Rivers Museum Catalogue, collected from the "Western Eskimo".

Bolas number 49 has six weights averaging 12 gm. The weights vary in shape from cylindrical to rectangular. Four are of bone, possibly walrus baculum; one is of walrus ivory; and one is of mammoth ivory. The lines are three-strand sinew twine, about 50 cm. long. There is a cluster of feathers, probably duck feathers, at the junction of the lines.

50. Belcher Collection, Museum no. P.R. 1018
    According to Pitt Rivers Museum Catalogue, collected at Icy Cape.

There are seven walrus ivory weights on this bolas. They average about 14.2 gm. and are roughly tapering trapezoidal blocks. One or two of the sides of each weight have a row of dots incised longitudinally. The lines are made of three-strand sinew, about 63.5 cm. long. A bunch of feathers is lashed at their junction with the lines.

Beluga and seal net

Nets for trapping belugas and seals were designed to be set perpendicular to the shore in ice-free water. Thornton probably saw a net of this type at Cape Prince of Wales in 1890 for he reported that sealskin nets were "astonishingly strong" and could hold an eight-hundred-pound bearded seal (*Erignathus barbatus*) or even a fifteen-hundred-pound beluga (*Delphinapterus leucas*), and that despite the animals' thrashing about, the net would drown them (Thornton, 1931:137-38). The nets were set offshore with large sinker stones and held afloat by inflated sealskins or bladders. One end was fastened to a large rock on the shore. Heavy stones were necessary to anchor these nets, so that they were very difficult to raise. The Eskimos would attach a line from the stone to an inflated sealskin float by means of a slipknot, and when the trough of a wave passed, they would take up the slack in order to raise the nets. In that way, when a large wave arrived, it would lift both the buoy and the rock. In 1890 at Cape Prince of Wales these nets took as many as ten bearded seals, twenty-four belugas and "considerable numbers" of harbour seals (*Phoca vitulina*) (Thornton, 1931:137-38, 179). The mesh size of beluga nets used by the Eskimos at Unalakleet was equal to the distance of "the tips of the extended thumbs placed together and the measurement taken on the palmar surface across both extended hands along the line of the thumbs" (Nelson, 1899:233).

Summer parties of travelling Eskimos carried seal and beluga nets with them. At Chamisso Island Beechey saw one such group, returning home to Cape Prince of Wales, carrying "some immense nets of hide made for taking small whales and porpoises" (Beechey, 1831, I:295). Rainey verified their use at Point Hope. He was told that:

> the upper edge of the net was suspended from a series of seal flipper floats attached by lines about 2 feet long. Its lower edge was weighted with bone sinkers which were also attached by lines. When a herd of beluga was seen approaching the net the watchers on shore threw stones behind and out beyond them to drive them into the net. Sometimes three or four were entangled at the same time. When one was caught, the hunters, armed with harpoons and lances, put out in a boat to spear the animal as it lashed about, entangled both in the net and the lines of the floats and sinkers. Occasionally an animal would disentangle itself after being harpooned, and tow a boat far out to sea. Walrus were sometimes caught in the beluga nets, and these were killed in the same manner. (Rainey, 1947:265)

51. Beechey Collection, Museum no. A.M. 687
Possibly collected at Cape Thompson, or at Point Jackson, Port Clarence; this specimen's label is ambiguous. (Fig. 28: A-C)

A

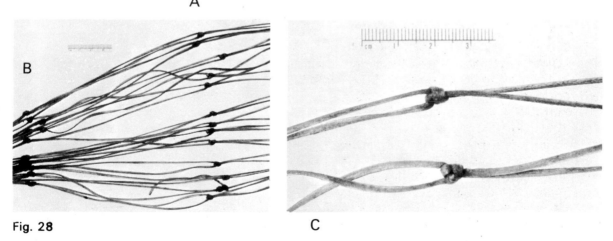

B

C

Fig. 28

This magnificent net is about fifty metres long and three metres wide. It is made from seal-skin line, approximately 2 mm. by 1 mm. The mesh is rhombic, 16 cm. on a side, and constructed with an ordinary mesh knot (Ashley, 1944:586, fig. 3791).

Net sinker

Net sinkers were used to keep a net in the proper position under water. They were usually of stone or whalebone and were lashed to the lower edge of the net at suitable places.

52. Belcher Collection, Museum no. P.R. 1700
  According to Pitt Rivers Museum Catalogue, collected at Icy Cape. (Fig. 29)

Fig. 29

The rock shown in figure 29 weighs about 2 kg., has no lashings, and is catalogued—probably correctly—as a net sinker. Beechey illustrated a similar rock in the sketches accompanying his hydrographic notes (Plate V). Judging from that sketch, it is likely that this sinker lost its lashings and became separated from its attachment toggle, which then was wrongly connected to number 70 (fig. 38). Nelson (1899:189, plate 70, 7) illustrated a stone net sinker from Point Hope that has lashings similar to those shown in Beechey's drawing. Because of its weight, it was probably used for a seal net rather than for a fish net.

Fish nets

Small-mesh fish nets of sinew or baleen fibre are well known from northwestern Alaska. Nets of this gauge could have been used primarily to take whitefish (*Coregonus* spp.) and herring (*Clupea pallasii*). Van Valin, who travelled extensively in northern Alaska in the early part of the twentieth century, wrote of these nets: "They are stretched across the mouths of streams and outlets of lakes, also set at right angles to the beach"; he added that "Sometimes the fish are so numerous that each and every mesh catches a fish at one setting" (Van Valin, n.d.:photo no. 62-2036-21). The nets could also be fastened, end-to-end, to others to increase their length. Baleen nets were in use in the Baillie Islands, east of the Mackenzie River delta until about 1890 (Stefansson, 1914:349).

A comment made by Bechervaise gives an indication of the price Beechey may have paid for his fish nets. Recalling an incident in 1826 near Point Franklin, he wrote,

> I recollect one of our officers offering several anchor buttons and small pieces of money for a whalebone net used to catch wild fowl, which was refused; sometime after meeting the man again, and desirous the officer should not be disappointed of his net, I offered him two white metal buttons from my jacket which was immediately accepted ([Bechervaise], 1839:208).

53. Beechey Collection, Museum no. A.M. 688
According to Pitt Rivers Museum Catalogue, collected at Port Clarence. (Fig. 30, A-C)

This fish net is about 6.25 metres long and about 70 cm. wide. Its meshing is made of two-strand caribou sinew. The twine is tied in a normal mesh knot (Ashley, 1944:586, fig. 3791) and the mesh is rhombic, about 2.5 cm. on a side. The edging lines are made of sealskin about 2 mm. wide. On the bottom line twenty-five sinker stones are attached at 25 cm.

Fig. 30

intervals. They are flat beach pebbles, lashed around the middle and joined to the bottom line with a baleen strip (fig. 30, c). The average weight of the stones is about 60 gm. The net has six spruce net floats, each about 15 cm. long, 6.5 cm. wide and 3.5 cm. thick. Each is lashed at both ends to the top line with baleen (fig. 30, b).

54. Beechey Collection, Museum no. A.M. 756
According to the 1836 Ashmolean Museum Catalogue, collected northeast of Icy Cape. Fig. 31, A-C)

This excellent specimen is too fragile to be unrolled, but it is estimated to be about twelve metres long. It is about 45 cm. wide. The net is made of baleen line, 0.5 mm. in thickness. The

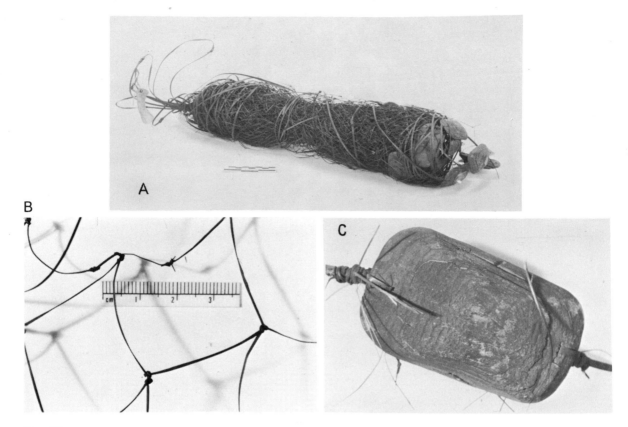

Fig. 31

mesh is rhombic, 3.5 cm. on a side. It is tied with an ordinary mesh knot. The edging lines are baleen strips, 3 mm. by 1 mm. About fourteen floats are attached to the net. The floats are bark chips about 7 cm. long, 3 cm. wide and 1 cm. thick. They are lashed at both ends to the top line with baleen. There are no sinkers attached to the net.

Ptarmigan nets

Ptarmigan (*Lagopus mutus* and *L. lagopus*) were widely taken in nets in northwestern Alaska. In the Point Barrow area nets were used more commonly by inland-dwelling Eskimos than by coastal Eskimos. After locating a flock, the hunters would set the nets to windward and then slowly drive the birds towards them. People who were flankers also helped to direct the birds' movements. Just before the birds reached the net, the drivers behind the birds would frighten them, forcing them to become entangled in the mesh (Sonnenfeld, 1957:131; Stefansson, 1914:388). Nelson reported that the birds could also be decoyed into the nets during the mating season. A hunter would erect a decoy at a conspicuous point and then surround it with the net. After taking cover, he would give out an imitation of a male bird's mating call. Often a male ptarmigan would fly directly to the spot to challenge the supposed intruder and would be trapped in the mesh. He illustrates one of these nets from St. Michael (Nelson, 1899:131-132, plate 51, 9).

Oquilluk (1973:99) reports that on Seward Peninsula November was the month in which ptarmigan were most commonly hunted. Charles Brower was another who witnessed the use of ptarmigan nets. As he described it, in the spring of 1885 near Kivalina

> the grouse were in immense flocks, and sometimes they came out in the open to feed on the small willow buds near the ground. The women would get their nets which were made of deer sinew braided. ... The nets were not over eighteen inches deep and were set up on the top of the snow, kept in an upright position with several small sticks; some of the nets were over a hundred feet long and would be set in a curve or at times a right angle. If there were many birds in a flock, several nets were set one to another stretching several hundred yards. The women and children would then get behind the flock and drive them slowly toward the nets. The ptarmigan would run ahead of them watching all the time and if the drive was not too fast, the whole flock at times would be entangled in the nets, the meshes of which were a little over four inches. The general name for nets is *co-bra*, but the grouse nets have a special name *po-o-au* (Brower, n.d.:157-58).

Brower also stated that in making the two-strand sinew, often a device like a flywheel would be used to help in the twisting. The sinew preferably came from the neck, back, shoulder blades or legs of the caribou. The sinew was cleaned and soaked before it was separated into strands (Brower, 1899:597).

Two nets acquired by Belcher are in the Pitt Rivers collections:

55. Belcher Collection, unnumbered. (Fig. 32, A-C)

The net is about twelve metres long and 32 cm. wide and is made of two-strand caribou sinew woven into an ordinary mesh knot. The meshes are rhombic, about 5 cm. on a side. The top and bottom lines are of three-strand sinew. The net was held up by six smoothed willow (*Salix* spp.) sticks, about 50 cm. long, spaced at roughly equal intervals. The bark is removed from all the willow sticks except one, which is broken and is lashed to a crooked piece retaining its bark.

Fig. 32 A B C

Fig. 33

56. Belcher Collection, unnumbered. (Fig. 33)

It is impossible to unroll this net because of its fragility, but it is estimated to be about 14 metres long. It is approximately 35 cm. wide. The mesh is two-strand caribou sinew tied in an ordinary mesh knot and formed into rhombic shapes 5 cm. on a side. The top and bottom lines are of three-strand sinew. The net was supported by seven willow stakes. The bark is removed from the sticks, and they are rubbed smooth. Each is about 40 cm. long.

Mesh gauge

Mesh gauges and netting shuttles were necessary for the manufacture of nets. Gauges allowed the proper length of twine to be set aside for tying and ensured uniform size. Shuttles made both the knotting and the twine storage more convenient.

57. Beechey Collection, Museum no. A.M. 752
Length, 29.1 cm. According to Pitt Rivers Museum Catalogue, collected from the "Western Eskimo". (Fig. 34)

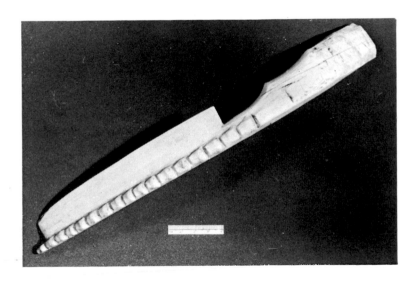

Fig. 34

The mesh gauge is made of walrus ivory. One edge has been crudely shaped into a number of dentate projections. The gauging blade is 16.0 cm. long which would produce a four-sided mesh of that dimension (Murdoch, 1892:312). This size mesh would have been intended for belugas and seals.

There are two mesh gauges in the British Museum's Belcher Collection (B.M. Nos. 8234-35, p. 101-105).

Netting shuttles

58. Belcher Collection, Museum no. P.R. 1525
    Length, 19.1 cm. According to Pitt Rivers Museum Catalogue, collected from the "Western Eskimo". (Fig. 35)

This netting shuttle collected by Belcher is made from walrus ivory. It has a deep longitudinal groove on each side to receive the netting twine.

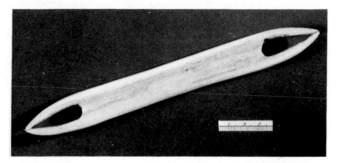

Fig. 35

Fig. 36

59. Beechey Collection, Museum no. A.M. 754
    Length, 45.7 cm. According to the 1836 Ashmolean Museum Catalogue, collected at Kotzebue Sound. (Fig. 36)

A netting shuttle of the size of number 59 would have been used to make large-gauge nets, probably for belugas and seals. This shuttle is spruce.

Cod and sculpin equipment

Winter fishing through the ice provided a steady source of food for the Eskimos of northwestern Alaska. Tom cod (*Microgadus proximus*), Arctic cod (*Boreogadus saida*) and sculpin (*Myoxocephalus* spp.) were taken near shore regularly (Sonnenfeld, 1957:146-148).

Fishing apparatus usually consisted of a winding rod and line. The line was often made of baleen because ice does not readily adhere to it, but it could have been made of other substances such as sinew, hide or the quills of gulls' feathers (Nelson, 1899:175). At the end of the line was a sinker, and hanging from that on one or more leaders were barbless hooks.

Murdoch witnessed and described fishing in the 1880s near Point Barrow:

> The fishing is carried on mostly by the women and children, though one or two old men generally go out, and one or two of the younger men, when they cannot go sealing and food is wanted at the house, will join the fishing party. Each fisherman is provided with a long-handled icepick, which he frequently leaves sticking in the snow near the fishing ground, a long line made of strips of [baleen], reeled lengthwise on a slender wooden shuttle about eighteen inches long and provided with a copper sinker and two pear-shaped "jigs" of walrus ivory armed with four barbless hooks of copper, and a scoop or dipper made of reindeer antler, with a wooden handle about two feet long. . . . Arriving at the fishing grounds, each proceeds to pick a hole through the ice, which is about four feet thick, clearing out the chips with the scoop. The "jigs" are then let down through the hole and enough line unreeled to keep them just clear of the bottom where the fish are playing about. The reel is held in the right hand and serves as a short rod, while the scoop is held in the left hand and used to keep the hole clear of the scum of new ice which, of course, is constantly forming. The line is kept constantly in motion, jerked up quickly a short distance and then allowed to drop back, so that the little fish that are nosing about the white "jigs" after the manner of codfish, are hooked about the jaw or in the belly.
>
> As soon as a fisherman feels a fish on his hook he catches up a bight of the line with his scoop and another below this with his reel, and thus reels up the line on these two sticks in loose coils till the fish is brought to the surface, when a skillful toss throws him off the barbless hook on the ice, where he gives one convulsive flap and freezes solid. The elastic whalebone line is thrown off the sticks without tangling, and paid out through the hole again for another trial. If fish are not found in plenty at the first hole the fisherman shifts his ground until he "strikes a school". They are sometimes so plenty that they may be caught as fast as they can be hauled up. One woman will frequently bring in upward of a bushel of the little fish . . . from a single day's fishing. The fishing lasts [from January] until about the middle of May, when the ice begins to soften (Murdoch, 1884:113-114).

Fishing gear similar to the Beechey and Belcher specimens was in widespread use throughout the Bering Strait region and northwestern Alaska in the nineteenth century (Bogoras, 1904:151, fig. 67; Nelson, 1899: plate 69; Nordenskiöld, 1882:575, figs. 7, 9, 11; Geist and Rainey, 1936: plate 22, *1, 2*). The spikes protruding from sinker number 62 were apparently designed as a further means of impaling nearby fish when the apparatus was jerked upward. The pieces of brass wire forming the hooks in number 63 are unique in the Beechey and Belcher collections. Although iron was not uncommon in northwestern Alaska during the 1820s, brass was probably scarce.

60. Beechey Collection, Museum no. A.M. 755
According to Pitt Rivers Museum Catalogue, collected northeast of Icy Cape. (Fig. 37:60)

This object is a line and storage rod assembly. The rod is made of spruce and is 43.0 cm. long. The line is composed of a number of tied baleen strips with a length of three-strand sinew twine included. The line could not be unwound from the rod, because of the fragile condition of specimen. It is estimated to be approximately 9.6 metres long.

61. Beechey Collection, Museum no. A.M. 789
According to Pitt Rivers Museum Catalogue, collected at Point Franklin. (Fig. 37:61)

This is a sinker to which a fishing line would have been attached. Made of walrus ivory, it weighs 370.5 gm., is 18.4 cm. long and has a light-coloured baleen lashing attached to the line hole at the top and to the leader holes at the sides. The side holes are gouged, but the line hole is drilled; it is 4 mm. in diameter.

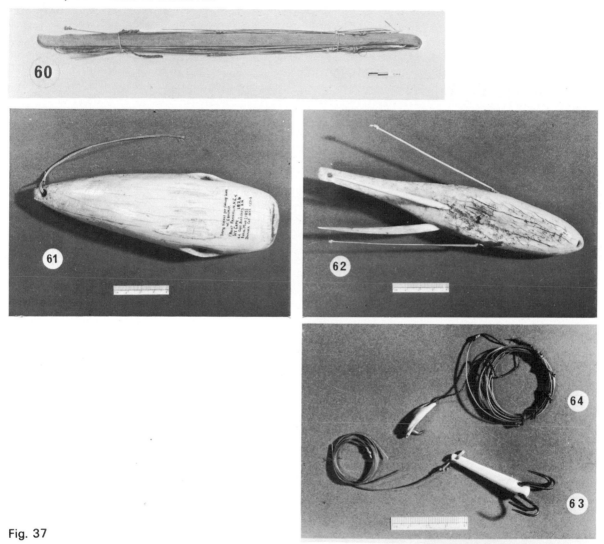

Fig. 37

62. Beechey Collection, Museum no. A.M. 787
    According to Pitt Rivers Museum Catalogue, collected at Point Franklin. (Fig. 37:62)

This sinker differs from number 61 in that it once had four spikes projecting upward. One spike is now missing and one is broken. The remaining spikes are each about 8.3 cm. long. The holes for the insertion of the spikes are drilled and are 4 mm. in diameter. Below the spikes are four drilled holes with plugs in them. Each plug holds the end of a baleen leader approximately 10 cm. long. Another hole at the bottom of the sinker may also have been for the attachment of a leader. The sinker is made from darkly patinated walrus ivory and weighs 153 gm. Its length is about 19.4 cm.

In view of the shape of this specimen, with its four projecting spikes, it may have been the archetype of the *manaktoun*, or seal retrieving hook, an implement developed for hunting seals with rifles. In rifle hunting, unlike harpoon hunting, there was no accompanying device for retrieving the quarry once it had been struck. The seal retrieving hook filled this need. It had the same pear-shaped body with spikes protruding from the point of maximum diameter that sinker number 62 has.

63. Belcher Collection, Museum no. P.R. 1700
According to Pitt Rivers Museum Catalogue, collected at Icy Cape. (Fig. 37:63)

Fish hook assembly number 63 consists of a baleen strip about 20 cm. long, an ivory shank 4.5 cm. long and four hooks made of two strips of brass wire passed through the shank.

Trout and grayling hook

64. Belcher Collection, unnumbered.
According to Pitt Rivers Museum Catalogue, collected at Icy Cape. (Fig. 37:64)

A baleen leader about 90 cm. long is attached to this fish hook assembly, and it is joined to about 9 cm. of three-strand caribou sinew. The shank of the hook is a seal's tooth, 2.5 cm. long. The hook is a small piece of iron, possibly a tack. A hook of this size could have been used to take Dolly Varden trout (*Salvelinus malma*), grayling (*Thymallus arcticus*) and sculpin (*Myoxocephalus spp.*) (Nelson, 1899:176-81). Similar hooks and leaders were employed on the Chukotsk Peninsula (Bogoras, 1904:150-51, fig. 67, *a,b*).

Burbot and sheefish equipment

Jigging for burbot (*Lota lota*) and sheefish (*Stenodus leucichthys nelma*)—larger and more voracious fishes than cod—was done in a manner similar to that used in cod fishing. Burbot and sheefish are found in the rivers of northern Alaska in the autumn and early spring and, because of the size of these fishes, the hooks are larger than those used for cod. Sinker-lures resembling small fishes are often used. In most other respects, the apparatus resembles cod equipment.

Fish hook assemblies similar to numbers 71 and 72 would have depended from sinker-lures such as numbers 65-70. The hooks were usually baited, but in the case of number 71 it is likely that the "head" was left exposed. Because of the smaller size of numbers 65, 66 and 70, they may also have been used as sinker-lures for small fish. In 1906 near the Mackenzie River delta, Faber reported seeing such a sinker-lure, in the shape of a fish, in use with a four-barbed hook (Faber, 1916:269).

65. Beechey Collection, Museum no. A.M. 788
Length, 8.5 cm. According to Pitt Rivers Museum Catalogue, collected at Point Franklin. (Fig. 38:65)

This is a sinker-lure, made from a mammoth tooth. There are gouged line holes at each end.

66. Beechey Collection, Museum no. A.M. 786
Length, 6.8 cm. According to Pitt Rivers Museum Catalogue, collected at "Behring Straits". (Fig. 38:66)

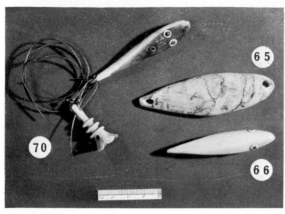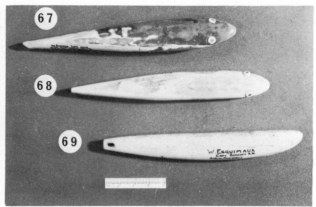

Fig. 38

In this sinker-lure inset baleen plugs are surrounded by ivory rings to represent eyes. The shank is ivory and is shaped like a small fish. There is a baleen plug inset to represent the anus. Gouged line holes are at each end.

67. Beechey Collection, Museum no. A.M. 782
    Length, 14.1 cm. According to Pitt Rivers Museum Catalogue, collected at "Behring Straits". (Fig. 38:67)

The varying hues of a piece of deeply patinated ivory have been cleverly used to represent a small fish in this sinker-lure. The eyes are made from what is possibly an inset piece of walrus whisker. Near the tail there are three other insets, probably of wood or baleen. Gouged line holes appear at both ends. The brown patina of the ivory in this piece probably came about from the ivory's having been long buried in a humic deposit.

68. Beechey Collection, Museum no. A.M. 783
    Length, 13.4 cm. According to Pitt Rivers Museum Catalogue, collected at "Behring Straits". (Fig. 38:68)

Like number 67, this sinker-lure uses the surface patination of long-buried ivory to approximate the colouration of a small fish; the eyes also are similar to number 67. An anal hole is represented by an inset of, possibly, bitumen. There are gouged line holes at both ends.

69. Beechey Collection, Museum no. A.M. 784
    Length, 13.0 cm. (Fig. 38:69)

This sinker-lure in general resembles number 67, but in this piece colouration comes from the granular core of a walrus tusk rather than from the dark patination of old ivory. The eye holes are also similar to those of number 67 except that the centres are probably baleen.

70. Belcher Collection, probably Museum no. P.R. 1700
    Length, 7.8 cm. According to Pitt Rivers Museum Catalogue, collected at Icy Cape. (Fig. 38:70)

The toggle on this sinker-lure probably was attached to the lure after its purchase. At one time it was the lashing toggle for net sinker number 52 (fig. 29). The sinker-lure is of patinated

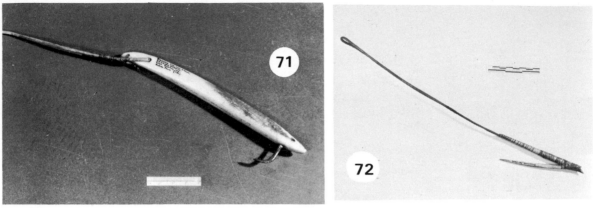

Fig. 39

ivory and made in a manner similar to that of number 67. On the dorsal surface are inset three blue beads about 3 mm. in diameter; two of these, which are designed to represent eyes, are rimmed with white ivory. A hole with a baleen inset represents the anus, and line holes are placed ventrally and at each end. A light brown baleen line connects the toggle and the sinker-lure.

71. Beechey Collection, Museum no. A.M. 781
Length, 15.7 cm. According to Pitt Rivers Museum Catalogue, collected at "Behring Straits". (Fig. 39:71)

The fish hook assembly seen in figure 39 has a baleen leader 35.5 cm. long, which is looped at both ends and lashed with sinew twine. The shaft of the hook-lure is made from dark-coloured ivory. It has incised line engraving to represent the gills and mouth of a fish. The eye has an inset lead rim surrounding, probably, a baleen centre. The hook is iron, more than 3 cm. long. Two line holes are drilled near the top of the shaft.

There is a similar hook-lure in the Belcher Collection of the British Museum (B.M. No. 8236, p.102).

72. Beechey Collection, Museum no. A.M. 778
According to Pitt Rivers Museum Catalogue, collected at Icy Cape. (Fig. 39:72)
Length, 42 cm.

This fish hook assembly is made of wood, baleen and bone. The bone barb is 12.2 cm. long, and the length of the leader and shaft is 41.8 cm. The leader is baleen, looped at the end and lashed, possibly with baleen. The shaft is wood, and a lashing, probably of bark, attaches the bone barb to the shaft.

Ice sieve

Ice sieves were useful in all winter fishing endeavours and are well known from northwestern Alaska and northeastern Siberia. An Arctic fisherman had to cut holes through thick ice to reach the fish below, and while he was fishing, thin new ice continuously formed. The fisherman used an ice sieve to remove small pieces of broken and forming ice from his hole. Because ice does not adhere easily to baleen, the mesh of the sieve was of that material, and to clear the accumulated slush from the mesh, the user needed only to strike the sieve against a piece of solid ice (Brower, n.d.:250).

Sieves similar to the Beechey sieve in the Pitt Rivers Museum are illustrated from Point Barrow (Murdoch, 1892:308), Kolyuchin Bay (Nordenskiöld, 1882:371) and St. Michael (Nelson, 1899:175, plate 67, *10*). The British Museum's Beechey collection contains one (no. 28/12-13/16) that is labelled as having come from Kotzebue Sound.

73. Beechey Collection, Museum no. A.M. 659
    Length, 130 cm. According to the 1836 Ashmolean Museum Catalogue, collected at Cape Thompson. (Fig. 40, A and B)

A

B

Fig. 40

This sieve has a spruce shaft 112 cm. long. The shaft widens near its junction with the rim, and in this widened area there is a triangular hole through which runs the sealskin line for lashing the shaft to the rim. In addition to this lashing there are two supporting lines, one on either side of the shaft, attached to the antler rim. The rim has a series of pairs of 2 mm. holes drilled at 2 cm. intervals to receive the baleen mesh. The sieve bowl is 25 cm. long and 23 cm. wide.

Snares

Nineteen snares collected by Beechey and Belcher are now at the Pitt Rivers Museum. Snares of this type were widely used by the Western Eskimos to trap ptarmigan (*Lagopus lagopus* and *L. mutus*) and ground squirrels (*Citellus parryi*) in a variety of situations. Nelson (1899:124, plate 51, *4*) purchased an identical snare from Cape Darby and reported that it would have been placed across the paths of ground squirrels with a bent willow or alder to act as a spring. In that same area such snares were also used in midwinter to trap ptarmigan (Oquilluk, 1973:99). Ptarmigan snares near Point Barrow were set over nests to catch the birds' legs (Murdoch, 1892:260); they were also set in a prepared fence of willow twigs through which the birds were driven (Sonnenfeld, 1957:161). Apparently a series of these snares could be very effective in producing food, for in April and May of 1870 a group of

Eskimos in the Mackenzie River delta took several hundred ptarmigan per day from the nooses (Bompas, n.d.:15). Van Valin gave this description of how snares were set:

> The snare is set at the mouth of the animal's hole in the ground on the runway. A thin pole or strip of [baleen] is pushed into the ground. Then the top of the snare is made fast to the end. The two sticks . . . are then driven into the earth . . . [and a line is stretched between them] over the hole or at right angles to the runway. The pole or [baleen strip] is then bent down until the opened loop of the snare is in the mouth of the hole or middle of [the] runway. Then the little wood button is slipped under the cross line and balanced sufficiently to hold the bent pole down and just enough to permit it to be jerked free when the animal runs his head through the noose. A crotched stick can be used instead of the cross string (Van Valin, n.d.:62-2036-102).

In manufacturing nooses for their snares the Eskimos near Unalakleet in the 1880s used a standard length of baleen strip that was equal to "the distance from the tip of the outstretched forefinger along the palm and inner side of the forearm to the point of the elbow" (Nelson, 1899:233). Some of the snares in Beechey's collection may have been the ones he saw when he went ashore north of Icy Cape in August of 1826, possibly near the village of Killimitavik (Beechey, 1831:I, 273; II, 673).

74. Beechey Collection, Museum no. A.M. 779 (Fig. 1:74)
    According to Pitt Rivers Museum Catalogue, collected from the "Western Eskimos".

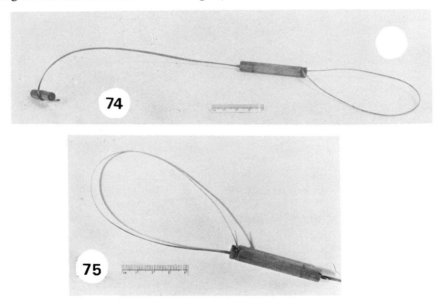

Fig. 41

Seventeen snares like number 74 were collected by Beechey. Each has a baleen strip about 50 cm. long which runs through a hollow tube 5.7 cm. in length. Where the strip emerges it is lashed to the tube. The other end of the strip is lashed to a short peg to aid in securing it. The tube is made from two semicylindrical halves of willow, one of which has a triangular groove cut in it, running the length of the semicylinder. The two halves are bound together with fine sinew strips.

75. Belcher Collection, Museum no. P.R. 1703 black. (Fig. 41:75)

Number 75 is one of two snares that are nearly identical to snare number 74. They differ only in that both halves of the tubes have triangular grooves.

Snow goggles

Snow goggles are a widely recognized and ancient element of Eskimo culture. They serve to prevent snow blindness by restricting the amount of light reaching the wearer's eyes. Goggles probably more than two thousand years old have been found in the Uelen-Okvik cultural sites near Cape Dezhnev at the eastern end of the Chukotsk Peninsula (Rudenko, 1961).

76. Beechey Collection, no. A.M. 700
    Length, 31.1 cm. According to the 1836 Ashmolean Museum Catalogue, collected at Cape Thompson. (Fig. 42)

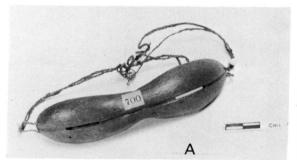
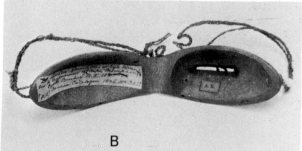

Fig. 42

The frame of these goggles is spruce, and at each end of the frame are two drilled holes about 1 mm. in diameter for the cord which holds the goggles on the head. The cord, fastened through the holes, is three-strand caribou sinew. The eye slits are 2.2 cm. long and 0.2 cm. wide. On the inside of the goggles, the area around the slits is blackened, probably to suppress glare, and probably accomplished through rubbing with soot. The outside of the goggles bears faint traces of red paint. There is a lightly incised black line running the length of the piece, connecting the two slits.

77. Beechey Collection, Museum no. A.M. 701
    Length, 14.5 cm. According to the 1836 Ashmolean Museum Catalogue, collected in West Georgia. (Fig. 43)

Fig. 43

These unfinished goggles are without the gouging for the nose and eyes. The frame is spruce and labelled as having come from West Georgia, a designation that Beechey applied to the Alaskan area north of Cape Beaufort.

Drag handles

Drag handles were used for hauling heavy weights, especially seals, over snow and ice. The handles were made in a variety of forms to accord with the use for which they were intended (Nelson, 1899:172). Handles with a bar-shaped toggle were often looped through an incision in the lower jaw of a seal's carcass for attachment to a man's dragging harness or a dog's harness line (Murdoch, 1892:256-58). Number 80 closely resembles a type of drag handle used by the Central Eskimos (Boas, 1888:481, Fig. 405).

78. Beechey Collection, Museum no. A.M. 780
    Length of toggle, 7.6 cm. According to the Pitt Rivers Museum Catalogue, collected from the "Western Eskimo" (Fig. 44, A and B)

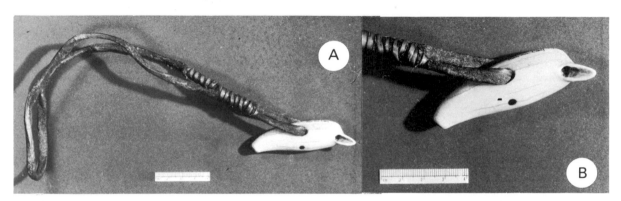

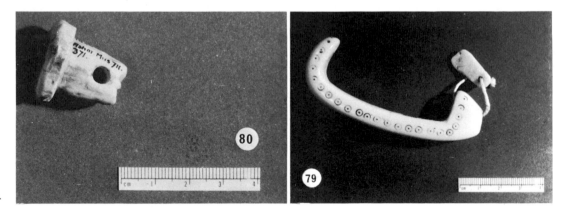

Fig. 44

The toggle on this drag handle is made of ivory and is carved to represent what seems to be a caribou's head. The eyes and nostrils are represented by holes drilled in baleen insets. The ear holes are drilled too, but lack insets. The line is a loop of bearded seal skin about 60 cm. long and 5 mm. square, which is formed into the loop by a seizing of baleen.

79. Beechey Collection, Museum no. A.M. 760
    Length, 8.9 cm. According to the Pitt Rivers Museum Catalogue, collected from the "N.W. Eskimo". (Fig. 44:79)

This crescent-shaped item is made of ivory and is decorated on the sides with incised circle-and-dot ornamentation. There is a gouged hole at one end, apparently for the insertion of a towing line. An ivory pendant of unknown purpose is attached; it was probably added after the handle was purchased.

80. Beechey Collection, Museum no. A.M. 711
    Length, 2.4 cm. According to the Pitt Rivers Museum Catalogue, collected at Point Franklin. (Fig. 44:80)

This carved ivory drag handle has the form of a T-shaped cylindrical plug. At its narrow end are four intersecting drilled holes, each about 4 mm. in diameter.

81. Beechey Collection, Museum no. A.M. 712.
    Length, 5.5 cm. According to the Pitt Rivers Museum Catalogue collected at Point Franklin. (Fig. 45, A and B)

Ivory toggle number 81 has an arc-shaped hole, about 5 mm. in diameter, on one surface.

82. Beechey Collection, probably Museum no. A.M. 713
    Length, 3.6 cm. According to 1836 Ashmolean Museum Catalogue, probably collected at Point Franklin. (Fig. 45, C and D)

This small toggle was carved from a walrus tooth and is very roughly made. Two gouged holes are pierced through it.

Inflation nozzle

Inflation nozzles are one of the most widespread items of Eskimo material culture. With an inflated float attached to a toggling harpoon head an Eskimo can take even the largest marine mammals—including the fifty-ton bowhead whale (*Baleana mysticetus*) and the Pacific walrus (*Odobenus rosmarus divergens*)—in most ice and water conditions. Without the float, the hunter was, for the most part, restricted to taking small seals. The reason for this is that an inflated float, by its drag in the water, serves to exhaust the animal. Macmillan's account of the use of floats in northern Greenland is particularly descriptive:

> Almost before the weapon has reached its mark the hunter is away with vigorous strokes of his paddle. The carefully coiled line whirrs from the deck as he retreats. The float ... [drops] into the water. We anxiously watch for motion, the signal that the game has been bagged. The float is violently jerked through the water, at times wholly submerged. The walrus is swimming deep and doing his utmost to escape from this strange enemy. . . .
>
> Rising to the surface, he glances at the black object persistently following. He turns, draws back his massive head and jabs repeatedly with his strong white tusks. The air-inflated skin rebounds like a rubber ball (Macmillan, 1927:188).

The first evidence of the use of inflation nozzles by Eskimos came from the Uelen-Okvik cultural site near Cape Dezhnev on the Chukotsk Peninsula (Rudenko, 1961). Larsen has traced its earlier use to northern Japan from where it apparently found its way into the Eskimo world (Larsen, 1968).

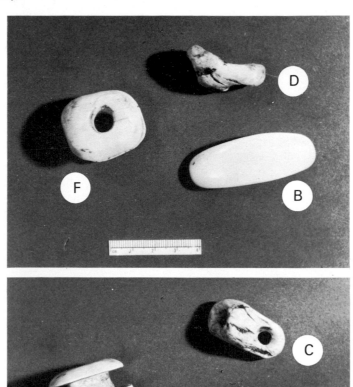

Fig. 45

83. Beechey Collection, Museum no. A.M. 710
     Length, 3.3 cm.; width, 2.9 cm.; thickness, 2.0 cm. According to the 1836 Ashmolean Museum Catalogue, collected at Point Franklin. (Fig. 45, E and F)

Float disc for whaling

When Froelich Rainey was excavating at Point Hope in 1940, he was told how float discs were used, and he presented this information in "The Whale Hunters of Tigara". Besides mentioning float discs, the passage quoted below gives interesting information about whaling:

Three floats were attached to each [whaling] harpoon line. Each float consisted of a complete sealskin with flippers attached. One large float (*kingu*) was fastened at the end of the line and two smaller floats (*kayasikkag*) were attached, side by side, a short distance ahead of it. The neck opening in each skin was tied over a small wooden shaft or toggle to render it air-tight. In addition, the *kingu* sometimes had a big wooden disc tied in the neck opening like a plug. Known as the *inyogluk*, this wooden plug had the face of a man or animal carved on it. When a whale escaped, dragging the floats after him, the *inyogluk* was supposed to call out and thus lead its owner to the wounded whale. Some [whaling captains] tied twigs to the *inyogluk*; when a stricken whale pulled the float beneath the surface of the water they said "the trees will grow large under the water and keep the whale from running away" (Rainey, 1947:257).

Nordenskiöld (1882:581, fig. 3) collected a piece at Port Clarence in 1879 that is nearly identical with the float disc acquired by Beechey.

84. Beechey Collection, Museum no. A.M. 753

Length, 13.2 cm.; width, 11.5 cm. According to the 1836 Ashmolean Museum Catalogue, collected at Port Clarence. (Fig. 46)

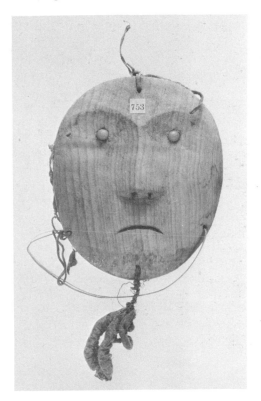

Fig. 46

This float disc[1] represents a human face; it is made of spruce and has two inset blue beads to indicate eyes. The beads are 9 mm. in diameter. Other features of the face are carved in low relief. A groove on the circumference of the disc has a two-strand sinew line in it. There are also three drilled holes on the face with sealskin or baleen lines in them. An unidentified object, apparently intestine, depends below the chin.

[1] Mrs. Dorothy Jean Ray kindly assisted with this identification.

Knives

Beechey observed during his voyage that iron, knives and other items of European or Asiatic origin were commonly in the possession of Eskimos of northwestern Alaska, and he assumed correctly that these had been obtained from the Chukchees of northeastern Siberia (Beechey, 1831:II, 576). Trade connections in fact extended much farther into North American than northwestern Alaska because Franklin in 1826 noted knives of Russian manufacture east of the Mackenzie River delta and Parry in the eastern Arctic in 1821-23 saw a double-edged knife that may have been like one of the two collected by Beechey. (Franklin, 1828:130; Parry, 1824:503-504).

Double-edged iron knives must have been both valuable and useful to the Eskimos, because copies were made in other materials: Nelson (1899:171-72, plate 65, *3*) on the northern side of Norton Sound, purchased a magnificent nephrite specimen in a shape similar to number 86; a slate piece in the shape of a halberd was found in the Uelen Cemetery near Cape Dezhnev (Arutiounov and Sergeev, 1969; 159) and Murdoch collected a slate copy of a double-edged knife near Point Barrow (1892:152, fig. 103).

Judging from the shape of the two Beechey knives they were made from halberds. Halberds were seen in the possession of Eskimos at Cape Thompson and at Grantley Harbour by Beechey, who recorded also that a group of Eskimos at Chamisso Island in September 1826 had a halberd that had been converted into a knife (Beechey, 1831:I, 264 and II, 298, 542). This shape persisted in Alaska for some time, well after iron had ceased to be an important part of the trade from Siberia. In the early 1880s, when whalers and traders were regularly visiting northwestern Alaska, Murdoch bought a sheet iron knife in the shape of a halberd and was told that it was "considered to be better than modern knives for keeping off evil spirits at night" (Murdoch, 1892:156, fig. 112).

There can be little doubt that knives of this shape were carried as much for self-defence as for use in hunting. In 1881 Captain Hooper noted that knives were worn under the shirt and could be "produced at any time without attracting attention by withdrawing the arm from the sleeve and taking the knife from the belt, so that when the hand reappears in the sleeve it holds the knife" (Hooper, 1884:106). Stefansson (1914:392) was told that a grooved knife with double edges was useful for human combat because it allowed blood to flow in the groove.

The knives in the Pitt Rivers collections may be two of the three Beechey removed from the natives' umiak after the shooting at Chamisso Island (see Appendix, p. 128-132).

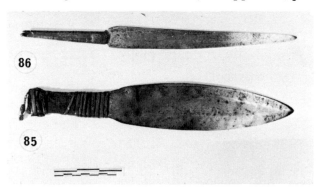

Fig. 47

85. Beechey Collection, Museum no. A.M. 765
    Length, 30.6 cm.; maximum width, 5.5 cm.; weight, 373 gm.; iron; according to the 1836 Ashmolean Museum Catalogue, collected at Kotzebue Sound. (Fig. 47:85)

86. Beechey Collection, Museum no. A.M. 766

  Length, 31.3 cm.; maximum width, 2.5 cm.; weight, 103 gm.; iron; according to Ashmolean Museum Catalogue (1836) collected at Kotzebue Sound. (Fig. 47:86)

Tools and Manufacturing Implements

A relatively large amount of iron is present in the Beechey and Belcher collections of the Pitt Rivers and British Museums, and its presence gives an indication of the availability of this material to the Eskimos in northwestern Alaska in the early nineteenth century. Members of the *Blossom*'s crew noticed that the Eskimos possessed iron and copper in quantity. In 1826 and 1827 these metals were not recent introductions to the region, for Captain Cook in 1778 had noticed iron spears at St. Lawrence Bay on the Chuktosk Peninsula (Beaglehole, 1966:411) and in 1816 von Kotzebue (1821:I, 252) found that the natives of the peninsula used three types of iron knives, one of which was two feet long. He was told on St. Lawrence Island that iron, beads and tobacco were traded to the islanders by the Chukchees in return for skins and he learned from the Chukchees that they obtained their items at Kolyma several hundred miles to the west (von Kotzebue, 1821:I, 251; II, 175).

The trade in iron across Bering Strait, which no doubt had been going on for more than a millennium, probably increased significantly after about A.D. 1675 by which time the Russians had established several trading posts near the Chukotsk Peninsula (Foote, 1965:3). In 1789 trading posts on the Lower Kolyma River began to operate, and as iron, copper, tobacco and beads became more readily available, the Chukchees became middle men, transporting American fox and marten furs and walrus ivory to the trading posts to the west and returning with tobacco, cloth, and copper and iron pots for the Americans. The Malemiut Eskimos carried some of these foods farther, trading them to the Indians of the upper Yukon River in return for furs (Ray, 1967:390). At about the time of Beechey's voyage Lütke found that the natives living on the coast of the Chuktosk Peninsula made annual trips inland to meet with the Interior Chukchees who had visited the trading posts (Lütke, 1835:II, 279-81). By about 1880 large numbers of sleds were making the journey from the eastern Chuktosk Peninsula to Kolyma and Anyui (Krause, 1882:30; Nordenskiöld, 1882:405).

It is probable that the range of trade goods from Siberia was still expanding within North America at the time of the first European contacts. Cook noticed that although iron was relatively common on the west side of Bering Strait, old barrel hoops were extremely valuable to the natives at Norton Sound (Beaglehole, 1966:438). In 1837 tobacco had not reached the Eskimos at Barter Island (Simpson, 1843:156), but eleven years later they were acquainted with it (Hooper, 1853:258). Similarly, labrets, which were not used east of the Mackenzie River in 1850 (Armstrong, 1857), were being worn as far east as Cape Bathurst less than twenty years later, at the time of Petitot's researches (1876:29; 1883:687).

One iron tool collected by Beechey was an adze with a heavy iron blade and at the time he obtained it—before iron had become readily available—it must have been of considerable value to its owner. A similar specimen was collected by Murdoch at Point Barrow (Murdoch, 1892:170, fig. 138). Belcher also collected an adze with a heavy iron blade (B.M. No. 8221, p. 101).

Adze

87. Beechey Collection, Museum no. A.M. 662
    Length, 33.2 cm. According to the 1836 Ashmolean Museum Catalogue, collected at Point
    Franklin. (Fig. 48)

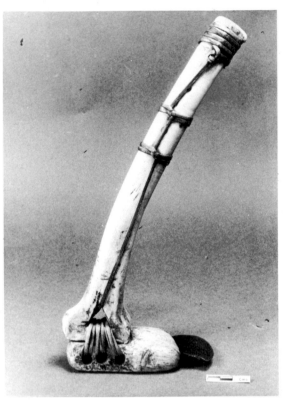

Fig. 48

The dimensions of the visible portion of the heavy iron blade of the adze shown in figure 48 are: length, 3.4 cm.; width, 6.5 cm.; maximum thickness, 9 mm. The blade is hafted in a whalebone head that has three lashing holes for attachment to the handle. The handle is 31.0 cm. long and made of caribou antler with a large triangular hole to receive the lashings from the head. The distal end of the handle has three drilled holes and at this end the handle has been split by sawing a dorsal-ventral groove running 18 cm. from the butt. The use of the groove and the holes is not known; perhaps the handle had some other, prior use. The head is lashed on with sealskin line which is then led down the handle and secured in a series of half hitches; this may have allowed ease in tightening the head lashings.

Pickaxe

Pickaxes were widely used by the western Eskimos. Nelson illustrated a specimen from Point Barrow that is nearly identical with the one acquired by Beechey, but Nelson labelled his an "ice pick" (Nelson, 1899:79, plate 35, *1*). Such implements no doubt had several uses. They were still in use in the 1890s at Cape Prince of Wales, where Thornton reported that they were used with scapula shovels to excavate house foundations and meat cellars (1931:149).

Froelich Rainey learned at Point Hope in 1940 that pickaxes with a narrow, pointed blade such as the one shown in figure 49 were often used as a root pick and that pickaxes with a spatulate blade were used for cutting sod blocks (Rainey, n.d.).

If the record of provenance for the pickaxe collected by Beechey is correct—that is, if it was collected at the northwestern extremity of Alaska, Point Barrow—then it must have been purchased by Thomas Elson in the *Blossom*'s barge on August 23, 1826.

88. Beechey Collection, Museum no. A.M. 660
    Length, 63.0 cm.; length of blade, 34.3 cm. According to the 1836 Ashmolean Museum Catalogue, collected at the N.W. extremity of Alaska. (Fig. 49)

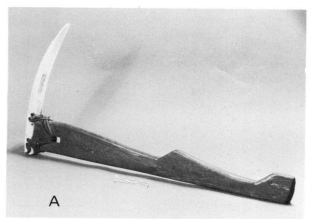 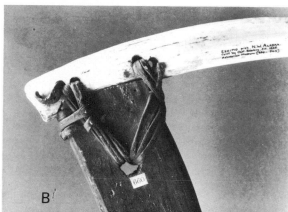

Fig. 49

The pickaxe has a spruce handle and an ivory blade. The blade has four drilled holes for the lashing line. The line is made from bearded seal skin. It is run through one large hole in the handle, and is seized to itself to increase tension in the lashing.

Blubber hook

Judging from the blubber hooks still in use at Point Hope, the type of hook shown in figure 50 was intended for carrying pieces of meat and blubber and was not used to help to dismember large marine mammals. Curiously enough, Ford found none of these hooks in his archaeological investigations of the Birnirk culture (ca. A.D. 500-800) near Point Barrow.

89. Beechey Collection, Museum no. A.M. 661
    Length, 68.5 cm.; length of hook, 18.8 cm. According to the 1836 Ashmolean Museum Catalogue, collected at Kotzebue Sound. (Fig. 50)

Fig. 50

The blubber hook collected by Beechey has a spruce shaft and an ivory barb. The barb is lashed to the shaft by baleen strips at three points. A similar blubber hook in the British Museum was collected by Belcher (B.M. No. 8237, p. 102).

Snow beater

Snow beaters were used to remove snow from skin clothing before a person entered a warm house. The snow had to be removed because wet skin clothing, especially caribou skin, rots, and this causes the hair to fall out, making the garment lose its value as an insulator. Nelson and Woldt illustrated specimens similar to Beechey's from Cape Prince of Wales (Nelson, 1899:77-78, fig. 21, *3*; Woldt, 1884:259, fig. 4).

90. Beechey Collection, Museum no. A.M. 751
    Length, 42.5 cm. According to the 1836 Ashmolean Museum Catalogue, collected at Point Hope. (Fig. 51)

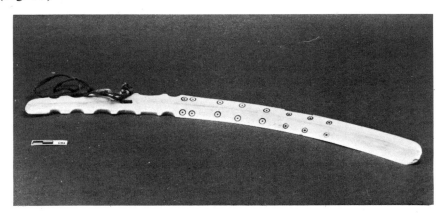

Fig. 51

The snow beater is a handsome specimen made of ivory. The handle has a series of crenellations for ease of gripping and there are deep medial grooves running the length of the object on each side. The spatulate blade is decorated with pairs of incised circle-and-dot designs. These pairs are placed on either side of the medial grooves; there are nine pairs on one side and eight on the other.

Boot sole creasers

Boot sole creasers were among the implements included in Eskimo women's tool kits. They were used to form the crenellations at the heel and toe of a boot sole and thus to give it high sides. Without a seam in the sole the boots were more waterproof. Belcher collected two boot creasers and both of them show similarities to creasers illustrated by Nelson (1899:plate 44).

91. Belcher Collection, part of Pitt Rivers Collection, unnumbered.
    Length, 11.9 cm. (Fig. 52:91)

Boot sole creaser number 91 is made of ivory, and the hilt is carved to represent an animal, probably a ground squirrel.

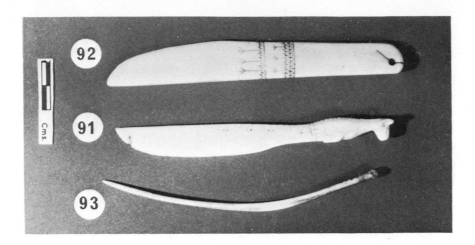

Fig. 52

92. Belcher, Collection, part of Pitt Rivers Collection, unnumbered.
   Length, 12.8 cm. According to Pitt Rivers Museum Catalogue, collected at Icy Cape.
   (Fig. 52:92)

Incised line ornamentation consisting primarily of lines and dentates decorates this specimen. A 2 mm. hole is drilled in the hilt. It is made of ivory.

Awl

Awls were used for piercing holes, much as they are today.

93. Beechey Collection, Museum no. A.M. 691
   Length, 11.6 cm. (Fig. 52:93)

Beechey's awl is made from a large bird's rib. It has a sharpened tip and was probably part of a woman's sewing equipment.

Sewing Kit

Eskimo skin clothing was made and repaired by women, and a sewing kit was a necessity. Collins (1937:351-54) has described the evolution of the shape of Eskimo needle cases and demonstrated that cases similar to the one collected by Belcher have their origins in the Old Bering Sea culture of St. Lawrence Island about 2000 years ago. From St. Lawrence Island cases of this type spread into the central and eastern Arctic of North America and probably were reintroduced into Alaska from the east sometime before A.D. 1400 (Ford, 1959:211-14; Giddings, 1952; plate 33, *3, 4, 9*; Larsen and Rainey, 1948:178).

94. Belcher Collection, Museum no. P.R. 1533
   Length of case, 8.0 cm. According to Pitt Rivers Museum Catalogue, collected at Icy Cape.
   (Fig. 53)

The sewing kit Belcher acquired consists of an ivory thimble holder with a carved representation of an animal head, a sealskin and bearded sealskin strip to hold needles, an ivory

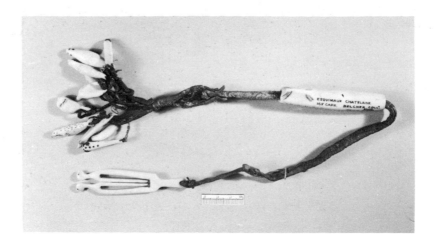

Fig. **53**

needle case with incised line and dentate decoration, and ten pendants. Two of the pendants represent seals, another one is a spotted seal, one is a stylized duck, and six are unidentified.

The needle case was designed to slide over the sealskin strip and thus enclose any needles that might have been inserted in it; it is similar to several needle cases illustrated by Boas (1906). The kit resembles two that were collected at St. Michael and on Norton Sound (Nelson, 1899:103-104, plate.44, *25, 33*). Because only some of the usual sewing equipment is included among the pendants—there is neither a creaser nor an awl—it is possible that this item was assembled for sale. Ornamental pendants were usually included in kits that were not made to be sold. The British Museum's Belcher Collection contains two sewing kits (B.M. Nos. 8212-13, p. 100) and five whetstones which probably were intended for inclusion in sewing kits (B.M. Nos. 8214-18, p. 100).

Fat removers

Fat removers were used to remove residual fat prior to drying and scraping skins to be cured. A scoop similar to number 95 was purchased by Nelson at Point Hope (1899:plate 50, *8*). It was used, he said, "by placing it in the palm of the hand with the grooved end resting against the inside of the fingers, the under surface against the palm, and pushing it from the operator" (Nelson, 1899:115). No specimens of close similarity to number 96 are described in the ethnographies of the area. Nevertheless, judging both from the variegated forms known to have been used and from the wear marks on the object's periphery, its assignation as a fat scraper seems justified.

95. Beechey Collection, Museum no. A.M. 750
    Length, 10.2 cm.; width, 5.8 cm. According to the 1836 Ashmolean Museum Catalogue, collected at Cape Thompson. (Fig. 54:95)

The fat remover designated number 95 is more a scoop than a scraper. It was carved from a piece of mammoth ivory and there are two small "horns" on the rim to aid in gripping it. A similar type was collected at the Diomede Islands by E.W. Nelson (Mason, 1901: plate 80, *2*). Beechey sketched an identical scoop in his hydrographic notes (Plate V).

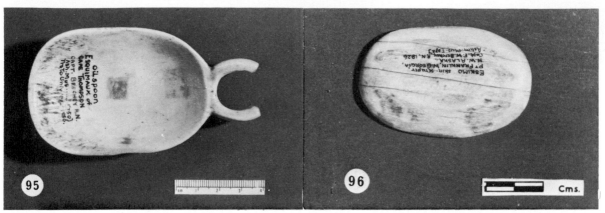

Fig. 54

96. Beechey Collection, Ashmolean Museum Catalogue, no. 372, probably Museum No. A.M. 714

Length, 6.3 cm.; width, 4.1 cm. According to the 1836 Ashmolean Museum Catalogue, collected at Point Franklin. (Fig. 54:96)

This oval disc was for scraping rather than scooping fat. It is made of walrus ivory and shows wear marks on the circumference.

Skin scraper

A scraper of the type would have been used by women for the final scraping and softening of skins. Similar specimens are known from Point Barrow, Sledge Island, St. Michael and Cape Darby (Mason, 1901:plate 73, *2* and plate 83, *2*; Murdoch, 1892:295, fig. 289; Nelson, 1899:133, plate 49, *11*; Hoffman, 1897:plate 35, *8*). The British Museum possesses a fine specimen closely resembling this one (Fagg, 1972:19, plate 12, *1*). The Belcher Collection of the British Museum contains two scrapers (B.M. Nos. 8219-20, p. 101).

97. Belcher Collection, Museum no. 1969.34.11

Length, 14.2 cm. (Fig. 55, A and B)

This skin scraper has a handsome mammoth-ivory handle and a chalcedony blade. The blade slot in the handle is drilled and gouged. The handle is 10.7 cm. long and has incised linear and circle-and-dot decoration. The blade is 6.4 cm. long, 3.8 cm. at its maximum width and 0.9 cm. thick. The distal edge of the blade shows wear marks.

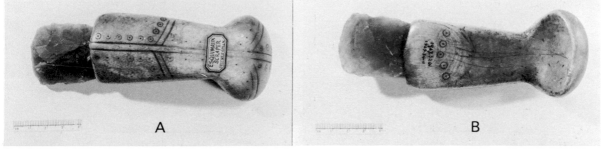

Fig. 55

Ladle

The ladle shown in fig. 56 is an impressive specimen that was given by Beechey to the famous geologist, the Rev. Dr. William Buckland, F.R.S. Buckland later donated it to the University Museum, Oxford. It is illustrated in Dr. Buckland's geological appendix to Beechey's narrative (Buckland, 1831:593-612, plate 1, *4*). It is made of mammoth ivory and has two incised lines running below the edge of the vessel and another two running the length of the handle. In the handle is a drilled hole 5 mm. in diameter. The lip on the distal edge shows wear marks.

This ladle may have been used as a dipper for drinking water. Simpson collected a similar one at Dease Inlet in 1837, and Ray, at Point Barrow, also collected a ladle of mammoth ivory (Simpson, 1843:148; Ray, 1885:plate 4, *6*). Murdoch felt that the latter two had been made in Kotzebue Sound and were then traded northward. He found them to be "rare and highly prized" (Murdoch, 1892:102-103).

Fig. 56

98. Beechey Collection, unnumbered. Probable Museum No. A.M. 750
Length, 27.7 cm.; width, 9.4 cm.; height, 6.2 cm. According to Pitt Rivers Museum Catalogue, collected at Cape Thompson and made from ivory from Eschscholtz Bay. Collected in 1827. (Fig. 56)

Spoon

99. Belcher Collection, part of Pitt Rivers Collection, unnumbered.
Length 13.2 cm.; maximum width, 2.9 cm. According to Pitt Rivers Museum Catalogue, collected at Icy Cape. (Fig. 57)

Fig. 57

The spoon shown in fig. 57 seems remarkable only in that it is made of ivory. A number of similar spoons of wood and horn are known from northwestern Alaska (Murdoch, 1892:104-105; Nelson, 1899:69, plate 30, 7). They were used for ladling soup and for filling lamps with oil. This specimen has a crude pattern of lines and dots incised on the handle.

Bag handle

Bag handles were attached to storage bags for ease in carrying.

100. Beechey Collection, Museum no. A.M. 697.
    Length, 41.5 cm., ivory. According to Pitt Rivers Museum Catalogue, collected at Kotzebue Sound. (Fig. 58)

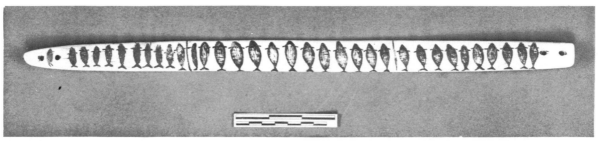

Fig. 58

The incised decoration in this handle is divided into three sections by vertical lines. In the middle section are thirteen whales, flanking which, on the right, are ten whales. In the left section are a group of ten whales and one walrus, or possibly a bearded seal. Two drilled line holes are at each end, each 4 mm. in diameter. The incised figures are probably blackened by rubbing with soot. Murdoch (1892:189-90) purchased a similar specimen, which is ornamented with representations of whales' flukes. He reported that the number of flukes on that bag handle represents the lifetime hunting tally of whales killed by one particular Eskimo whaling captain from Point Barrow.

Drill mouthpiece

Mouthpieces like the one shown in fig. 59 were used to brace a drill shaft and to provide pressure on the bit. Holding a drill shaft with a mouthpiece left the operator's hands free to guide the drill's bow and to secure the object that was being worked on.

Fig. 59

101. Beechey Collection, Museum no. A.M. 698
     Length, 11 cm. According to the 1836 Ashmolean Museum Catalogue, collected at Kotzebue Sound. (Fig. 59)

A grey stone socket piece, possibly of chert, is inset into the spruce frame of this mouthpiece. There are breathing holes on both sides of the bit.

Belcher collected two mouthpieces which are in the British Museum's collection (B.M. Nos. 8207-08, p. 100).

Drill bows

Bow drills were used regularly by Eskimos in northwestern Alaska (Murdoch, 1892:76; Nelson, 1899:plate 37). They are still used today by ivory carvers. The bows were used with a drill shaft, bit and mouthpiece (see no. 101) to produce rapid turning of the bit. The use of a bow with its line wrapped around the drill shaft allowed increased speed of rotation compared to other methods, and it freed one of the driller's hands, enabling him to hold firmly the object being worked on.

Drill bows are one of the most widely admired objects of Eskimo material culture because of their intricate and elaborately engraved designs. More than on any other object, Eskimo engravers invested large amounts of time in decorating their drill bows. Nelson wrote a thorough description of how the bows were manufactured:

> The tusk selected was rudely scratched with a fragment of quartz, or other siliceous stone, along the length of the tusk until the sharp edge would no longer deepen the groove; the other three sides were scratched or channeled until the pieces of tusk could be separated. Sometimes this was done by pressure of the hand, or effected by means of a knifeblade-shaped piece of wood, on which was struck a sharp blow, and so skilfully dealt as not to shatter or fracture the piece intended for use. The other side or slabs, were removed in a similar manner.
>
> The piece intended for drill bow or other use was now scraped (rubbed) with a fragment of freshly broken basalt. . . . The holes or perforations in the ends were produced by means of stone drills after a depression had been made by an angular piece of stone. . . . A few grains of sand were put into the shallow cavity and the stone drill started. . . .
>
> The final smoothing of the surface of the ivory piece was effected by rubbing it against a fine-grained stone or in the hand where fine sand was held; lastly two pieces of ivory were rubbed against each other and thus a polished surface produced.
>
> The etching was done with sharp edges of fragments of flints. Sometimes these stone fragments were skilfully fastened into a piece of wood and used as gravers or even as lancets.
>
> The drill bow or other implement or utensil was not produced in a day or even in a month, as these articles were usually created for personal use. I have known of such articles being taken along while on a protracted hunting expedition and there worked upon to while away the oftentimes tedious hours of watching game. Again I have known when a native had requested a friend to etch some design, and in their festivals, commemorating their dead, these articles were often presented and highly cherished as gifts (Nelson, 1897:774-75).

Curiously enough, drill bows with the type of incised decoration seen on the Beechey and Belcher specimens are a recent addition to Western Eskimo material culture. This style of engraving was not known before A.D. 1200 and the florescence of engraved bows was primarily a nineteenth-century phenomenon (Ray, 1969:11). In comparing Beechey's and Belcher's specimens to later drill bows, Ray (n.d. b) has observed that the Beechey and Belcher drill bows, which are among the earliest such objects collected by Europeans, are notable for the absence of representations of dog teams, Europeans and ships and are distinguished by the depiction of a high proportion of mythological creatures. The lack of dog teams on the drill bows may be explained by the fact that the growth of the fur trade—and the concomitant increase in dog traction for tending trap lines—occurred later in the nineteenth century; but, as Ray (n.d. *a*) has suggested, the lack of Europeans and ships is puzzling, judging from the number of native-European contacts prior to Beechey's voyage.

102. Belcher Collection, Museum no. 1969.34.9
Length, 32.8 cm.; walrus ivory. (Fig. 60)

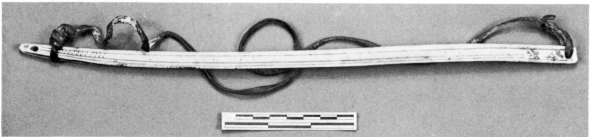

Fig. 60

This drill bow is an unfinished specimen. Apart from some line-and-dentate ornamentation and apart from the sketches of what may be representations of two caribou heads, it is not decorated. The bow retains its sealskin line.

103. Beechey Collection, Museum no. A.M. 692
Length, 40.3 cm.; walrus ivory. According to Pitt Rivers Museum Catalogue, collected at Kotzebue Sound. (Fig. 61, A-D)

Side A of the drill bow depicts, left to right, two men dragging a bearded seal and five umiaks engaged in a walrus hunt. Side B from left to right shows two umiaks and three men, possibly hunting a bear on sea ice, and mythological creatures with men who may be shamans. This is followed by a scene of what may be an Eskimo athletic contest. Farther to the right a number of figures are dragging seals and hunting; at the far right is a dancing scene. Side C is divided into two parts: on the left, a whaling group with migrating birds and, on the right, a scene with an empty umiak and six men bending at the waist. Side D begins, from the left, with a whale and an umiak, and then two kayaks. In one of the kayaks a man is throwing a bird spear at a group of birds. This is followed by a wrestling scene and by what appears to be some women preparing to butcher seals.

104. Beechey Collection, Museum no. A.M. 694
Length, 31.8 cm.; walrus ivory. According to Pitt Rivers Museum Catalogue, collected at Kotzebue Sound. (Fig. 62, A-D)

The drill bow is also of walrus ivory and exhibits exceptionally skilful carving. Side A begins at the left with, apparently, two men hunting bears with bow and arrow. A village scene with dancing figures follows. After that there is a representation of a dance house, or *kazgi*, which includes dancing figures and possibly a shaman in flight. Following in succession are houses and meat caches, a caribou, two men dragging seals, an archer hunting a group of caribou, and a man dragging a seal toward a group of houses and meat caches. Side B, for the most part, shows umiaks under paddle and sail. Two sizes of umiaks are depicted: the large ones used for travelling and the small ones used for whaling and walrus hunting. Some dogs or wolves are shown, and there is a group of figures—some with walking staves—and a scene of a

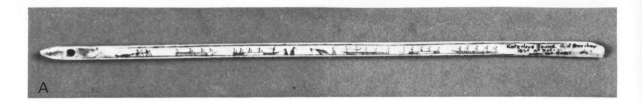

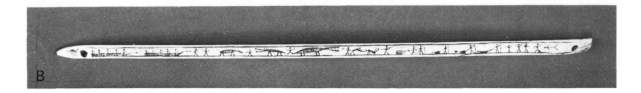

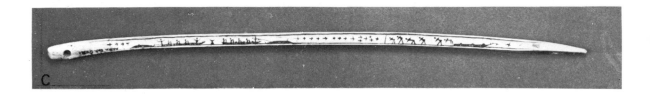

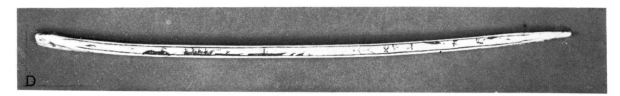

Fig. 61

man spearing walrus in the water. On side C, beginning from the left, there is depicted a winter house, an unidentified object, an umiak on its side with a man, an unidentified figure, a kayak on a rack and a man, another man, a caribou, three cranes, a dog, another crane, and unidentified figures. These are followed by a large seal or bearded seal, men dancing, a ground squirrel in a snare trap, some unidentified figures, and two people in a low house. To the right are an animal with an unidentified object in its mouth, four men in an umiak, three men dragging a large seal, and two other men dragging seals. Side D shows a crane, skins hanging from a rack, people possibly cooking, caribou entering the water and men spearing them from kayaks, a group of people with *paamerak*-type houses (see p. 123), skins and fish on drying racks, possibly a bear on its haunches eating the fish, some unidentified lines, and caribou grazing and swimming.

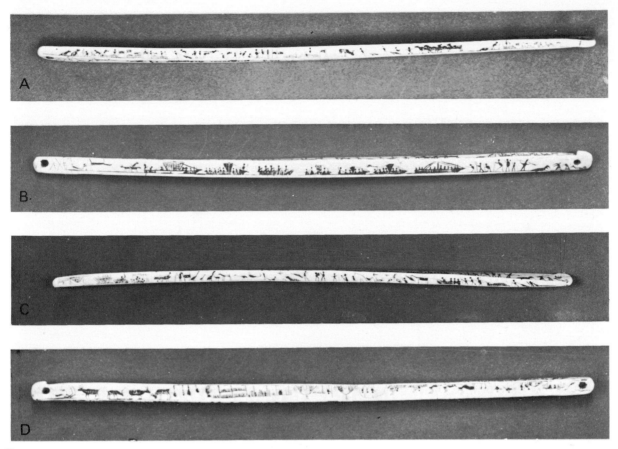

Fig. 62

105. Beechey Collection, Museum no. A.M. 693
    Length, 35.3 cm.; walrus ivory. According to Pitt Rivers Museum Catalogue, probably collected at Kotzebue Sound. (Fig. 63, A-D)

    Side A of this drill bow, from the left, shows an unidentified animal followed by, apparently, an empty umiak and then four people sitting and smoking. One of the men, seemingly with a pipe in his hand, is reeling backward from the strength of the tobacco (Ray, n.d. *b*). This scene is followed by three figures probably dressed in costumes to imitate caribou. An unidentified section is followed by two human figures with raised arms, and then an elevated line on which are basking seals and possibly some dancers. At the right are more human figures and caribou. Side B, from the left, shows houses and human figures, a man pulling a harpooned animal from the water, a man dragging a seal, a mythological or dancing figure, an umiak, a bird on a rock, several men in kayaks, and houses. Side C shows three figures with a fence and caribou snares, flying birds and men in an umiak. A camp scene follows, with meat and fish drying on racks, a tent and woman cooking in front of a fire, more human figures and a dog. Next is a man stalking caribou and a bird—possibly a mythological creature—above a harpooned whale. Caribou are the primary subject of side D; there are also one hunter and, in the far right, apparently the figures of a woman and child in front of tents and fish-drying racks.

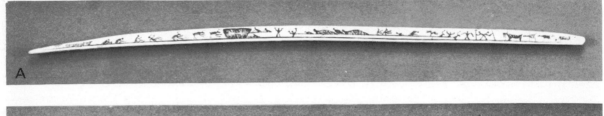

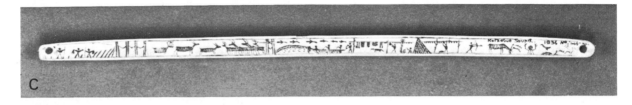

Fig. 63

106. Beechey Collection, Museum no. A.M. 695
     Length, 36.3 cm.; walrus ivory. According to Pitt Rivers Museum Catalogue, collected at
     Kotzebue Sound. (Fig. 64, A-D)

This drill bow is carved in a cruder style than the others. Side A, from the left, shows caribou amid trees. An animal, possibly a weasel or marten, is next. There is also a man in a kayak spearing a swimming caribou and another figure of a swimming caribou. A man dragging a kayak over ice on a small sled follows, and then another figure of a marten or weasel. After this come a seal and walrus, apparently basking on ice; a man in a kayak throwing a harpoon at them; a tent with a man and a dog; and a man and a dog dragging a large sled. Side B shows a bearded seal and an umiak that has an object, probably a hunting charm, hanging from the bow. A similar pendant is shown in Wolfe's sketch of Eskimos offering trade goods from an umiak (Plate II). A whale is next, followed by a scene of two umiaks harpooning another whale; then a human figure holds two walruses by lines, and the figure of a marten or weasel is included. On the right there are five dancing figures. Sides C and D depict many sitting or swimming animals, probably caribou.

107. Belcher Collection, Museum no. P.R. 15/12395
     Length, 35.2 cm.; walrus ivory. (Fig. 65, A-C)

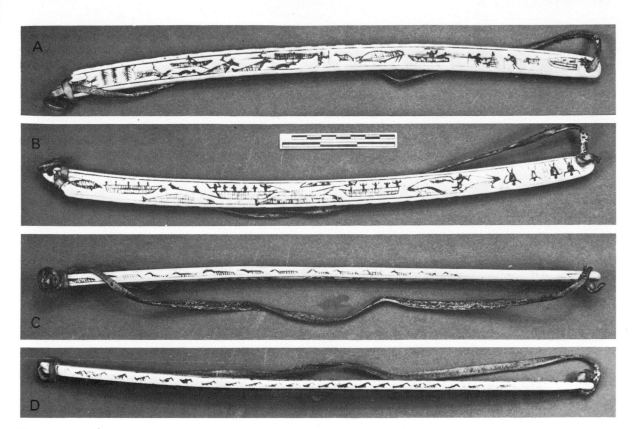

Fig. 64

This bow is triangular in cross section. From the left side A depicts men and dogs driving caribou, possibly toward a corral. Farther to the right are grazing caribou, two hunters—one of them with dogs—and some lying caribou. Side B shows migrating and grazing caribou. Side C has, from the left, seven caribou, then a village scene with houses and caches. This is followed

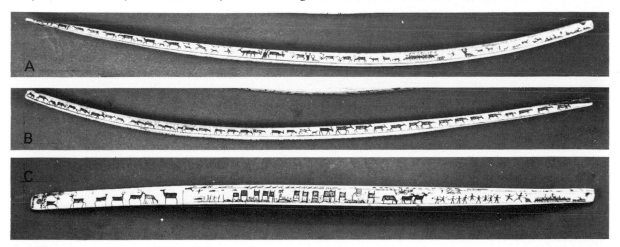

Fig. 65

by what is probably a scene of people driving caribou into a corral and then into a river where they are being speared by a man in a kayak. Above this are more scenes of caribou and men in kayaks.

108. Belcher Collection, Museum no. P.R. 2794
Length, 37.7 cm.; walrus ivory. According to Pitt Rivers Museum Catalogue, collected between Icy Cape and Point Barrow. (Fig. 66, A-D)

Side A of this drill bow shows, from the left, several unidentified objects, then two wrestlers, an unidentified object, a dancer or mythological creature, three caribou, two unidentified objects, two wrestlers or dogs, an umiak and possibly three dogs, an unidentified object, two walruses, two men and two mythological creatures and one man. Side B has some unidentified objects at the left followed by a scene of an umiak and a harpooned whale. These are followed by two wrestlers and then a number of dancers or, possibly, a mythological scene. Then there is an umiak and paddlers and several caribou being attacked by hunters, followed by five human figures. Side C depicts a number of figures of men and dogs near a hill or house, two unidentified figures, two umiaks and harpooned whales and some unidentified figures, then several figures of men and caribou, an unidentified object and probably a beluga. Side D is primarily composed of swimming caribou and men in kayaks spearing them. There is also the figure of a whale.

The British Museum's Belcher Collection also contains two drill bows (B.M. Nos. 8209-10, p. 100).

Fig. 66

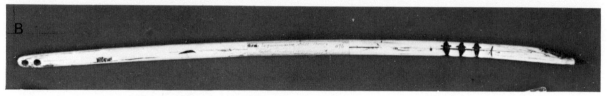

Fig. 67

109. Beechey Collection, Museum no. A.M. 696
    Length, 39.6 cm.; walrus ivory. (Fig. 67, A and B)

The bow is probably unfinished and it has been only sparsely decorated. Side B depicts three whales, and there are some unidentified figures.

OTHER ARTEFACTS

Labrets

Labrets like those shown in Fig. 68 were used to prepare a young man's lip for the insertion of a full-sized labret. Beechey (1831:I, 249) recorded that the diameter of the hole began at about "the size of a quill" and that it was gradually enlarged until it was a half inch in diameter and could be stretched to three-quarters of an inch. He mentioned seeing some in use at Point Lay on August 20, 1826:

> The males of this party were all provided with lip ornaments; and we noticed a gradation in the size, corresponding to the ages of the party who wore them, as well as a distinction in the nature of them. Two young lads had the orifices in their lips quite raw: they were about the size of a crow-quill, and were distended with small cylindrical pieces of ivory, with a round knob at one end to prevent their falling out. For some time after the operation has been performed, it is necessary to turn the cylinders frequently, that they may not adhere to the festering flesh. . . . In the early stage it is attended with great pain, the blood sometimes flowing, and I have seen tears come into the boys' eyes while doing it (Beechey, 1831:I, 280).

In the 1890s Brower witnessed their use near Point Barrow:

> Every man and boy over 14 had these labrets. When a boy approached 13 or 14 he always had both sides of his lower lip pierced by some medicine man. They used in the old days to use a flint chip, placing inside the lip a small piece of wood, then jabbing a small hole. This was enlarged until some of them could get a labret through the hole at least one and a half inches long.
>
> Labrets were of every material and every shape. Most were stone; some were ivory, some lignite, some hard bitumen, amber, turquoise marble; in fact, anything that took their fancy. Even the glass stoppers from bottles were of use (Brower, n.d.:489-90).

Some labrets were very large; Beechey bought one of polished jade (nephrite) that was 3 inches by 1½ inches. Belcher sketched a similar labret in his journal (plate VII). Two labrets of this type are in the British Museum's Belcher Collection (B.M. Nos. 8205-06, p. 100). At

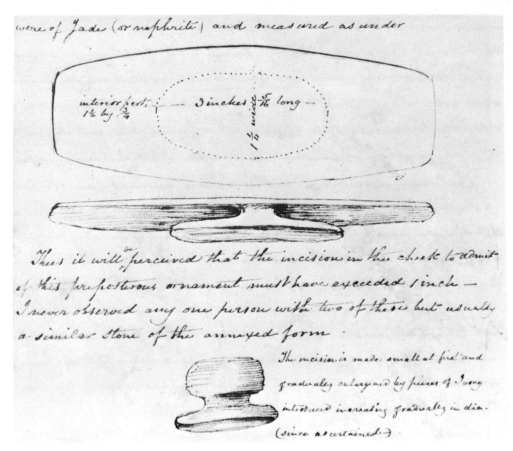

were of Jade (or nephrite) and measured as under

interior part: 1½ by ¾ — 3 inches ⁵⁄₁₆ long —

Thus it will be perceived that the incision in the cheek to admit of this preposterous ornament must have exceeded 1 inch — I never observed any one person with two of these but usually a similar stone of the annexed form.

The incision is made small at first and gradualy enlarged by pieces of Ivory introduced increasing gradualy in dia. (since ascertained)

Plate VII Belcher's sketch of labrets from his Journal. By courtesy of the University of British Columbia Library.

Hotham Inlet on July 22, 1826, Beechey met several umiaks with from ten to thirteen men in each, all of whom wore labrets. These were either of ivory, ivory with blue beads attached, or of stone: steatite, porphyry, or greenstone (Beechey, 1831:I, 250). Beechey noted that the Eskimos readily disengaged the labrets from their lips

> and sold them, without minding the inconvenience of the saliva that flowed through the badly cicatriced orifice over the chin; but rather laughed when some of us betrayed disgust at the spectacle, thrusting their tongues through the hole, and winking their eyes (Beechey, 1831:I, 250).

The use of labrets is known to have extended from western Alaska as far east as Cape Bathurst in the Northwest Territories (Petitot, 1876). Murdoch has suggested that the practice of wearing labrets east of the Mackenzie River was relatively recent, and he quoted Armstrong (1857) who said that in 1850 none were being worn in that area. Nevertheless, by the time of Petitot's (1883:687) and Bompas's (n.d.) journeys in the 1860s and 1870s, they were widely worn in the Mackenzie River delta and east of there.

In 1816 Kotzebue and Choris both noted the use of large blue beads for attachment to labrets (Plate VIII) and prior to their voyage, as Murdoch surmised, the beads, like iron, must have been traded across Bering Strait from Siberia (Kotzebue, 1821:I, 210; Choris, 1822, plate 2). By the early 1880s the use of large stone labrets had gone out of use (Murdoch, 1892:146-147).

Plate VIII Watercolour and ink sketch by Louis Choris of Eskimos at Shishmaref Inlet, 1816. By courtesy of Yale University.

Labrets were used with a number of other items for facial adornment. Choris depicted several natives of Shishmaref Inlet with beads suspended from their ears and from brow bands (Plate VIII). Beechey noted that beads were hung from the ears of the Eskimos at Hotham Inlet and at Chamisso Island he saw a woman with a piece of baleen through the septum of her nose and a blue bead dangling from it (Beechey, 1831:I, 250, 287). These decorative practices continued for at least another half century, when Rosse reported a woman at Cape Blossom in 1881 with a "bunch of beads suspended from the septum of her nose" (Rosse, 1883:36).

Certain types of beads had great value. In his autobiography Brower (n.d.:147) reported that in the winter of 1884-85 an impoverished Eskimo arrived at Point Barrow with only one blue bead. He traded this for a sled and five dogs, ten slabs of baleen, five cross-fox skins and one silver-fox skin: goods that Brower valued at more than one thousand dollars.

Each of the ten labrets collected by Beechey (fig. 68) differs in the size of its shaft diameter.

110. Beechey Collection, Museum no. A.M. 760a
Length, 1.8 cm.; walrus ivory. According to Pitt Rivers Museum Catalogue, collected from "N.W. Eskimos". (Fig. 68)

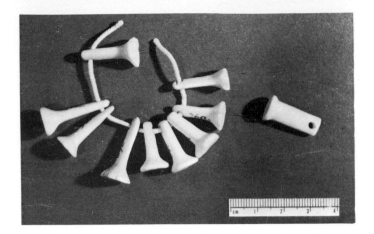

Fig. 68

There is a similar set of labrets in the British Museum's Belcher Collection (B.M. No. 8196, p. 99). That collection also contains eight other labrets in a variety of shapes and materials (B.M. Nos. 8197-8204, p. 99).

Ivory chain

It has not been possible to determine the use of the ivory chain collected by Beechey. Perhaps, like the ivory chains found in the Ipiutak culture graves at Point Hope, this was a shaman's item of equipment. Chains are known to have been used by shamans also in northeastern Siberia (Larsen and Rainey, 1948:131). Wolfe mentioned that ivory chains were bought from the Eskimos at Chamisso Island on August 29, 1826 (Wolfe, n.d.:130).

111. Beechey Collection, Museum no. A.M. 749
       According to Pitt Rivers Museum Catalogue, collected at Eschscholtz Bay. (Fig. 69)

The specimen is composed of eighteen links of mammoth ivory, each about 5.6 cm. long.

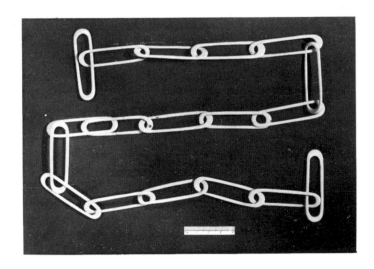

Fig. 69

Model lamp

Lamps were used throughout the Eskimo world to provide both light and heat by the burning of animal oils, primarily sea mammal fats. Because soft stone for lamps was not locally available in northwestern Alaska, this material was imported across a great distance from the Coronation Gulf area of the Northwest Territories of Canada. The Eskimos of that region supplied stone to most of the Eskimos of the western Arctic of North America and, possibly, of northeastern Siberia as well (Stefansson, 1914:27).

112. Beechey Collection, Museum no. A.M. 762
Length, 16.7 cm.; weight, 472 gm. According to the 1836 Ashmolean Museum Catalogue, collected at Kotzebue Sound. (Fig. 70)

Fig. 70

The soapstone lamp seen in figure 70 was probably a girl's toy. Nelson recorded that Eskimo girls had "small models of dishes and other women's household utensils" (1899:331). In form it resembles a full-sized lamp collected at Point Barrow in the 1880s (Hough, 1898:plate 11, *1*) and it closely corresponds to lamps used throughout northwestern Alaska (Murdoch, 1892:106, fig. 47). Its transverse ridge would have been used to support a moss wick.

This specimen has two small holes drilled through it, and these are plugged with wooden pegs. This suggests that the soapstone from which the lamp was carved had originally been a larger vessel, probably one that had broken. The position of the holes suggests that they were intended for the attachment of suspension cords, and therefore, that the broken fragment may have been a piece of a cooking pot.

Model sledge

Like the miniature lamp (no. 112), this model sledge was probably a child's toy.

113. Beechey Collection, Museum no. A.M. 770
Length, 22.2 cm.; width, 11.1 cm. According to the 1836 Ashmolean Museum Catalogue, collected at Kotzebue Sound. (Fig. 71)

This model is made of spruce. It probably represents the type of small sledge used for dragging pieces of meat and blubber and other small objects for short distances.

Fig. 71

Rain shirts

Rain shirts made of intestines are well known among the western Eskimos, and many observers have praised their lightness and water-resistant qualities. Peard and Wolfe recorded their comments about these when the *Blossom* was off the southwestern corner of Saint Lawrence Island on July 17, 1826:

> [The Eskimos] wore a water-proof shirt made of [walrus] gut, which is cut into strips of about 6 inches wide, sewn together horizontally & puckered so as to resemble very much the sleeves & flounces that were, & perhaps are now so fashionable amongst the English ladies (Peard, 1973:146).

> They had several 'kamlaikas' a sort of shirt made from the intestines of the whale, walrus, or seal, some almost as fine as gold beater's skin, they are secured with sinews and being well oiled, become completely waterproof (Wolfe, n.d.:110).

Nelson (1899:36) stated that in western Alaska the gut strips were sewn together horizontally, but Ford (1959:220, fig. 106a) has illustrated a rain shirt excavated from the Birnirk site near Point Barrow that has a vertical arrangement of the strips.

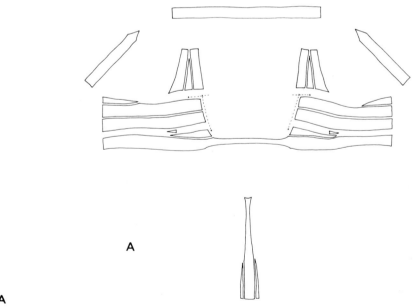

A

Fig. 72A

Both Nelson (1899:36) and Murdoch (1892:122) mentioned that the seams on rain shirts were reinforced with a black or coloured filament. In the 1880s at Point Barrow this was done with cotton thread, but at the same time in western Alaska "seals' bristles or the fine hair-like feathers of certain waterfowl" were used (Nelson, 1899:37). It seems that apart from the ornamental aspects of this practice, the use of the organic material in the stitching helped to increase the water resistance of the seams.

114. Beechey Collection, Museum no. A.M. 655
   Length, 86 cm. According to the 1836 Ashmolean Museum Catalogue, collected at Kotzebue Sound. (Fig. 72, A-C)

The seams of this rain shirt are sewn with a stitch[2] that zig-zags through both layers of the two intestine strips.

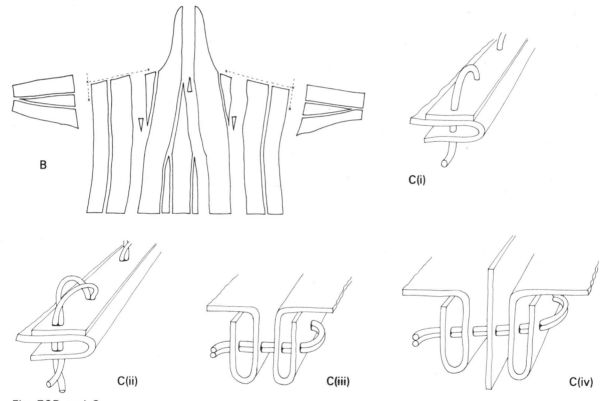

B

C(i)

C(ii)   C(iii)   C(iv)

Fig. 72B and C
   Details concerning Figure 72.
A. Gut components of the front and sides of the rainshirt.
B. Components of the back of the same.
C. Stitching used in no.114.
   (i and ii) Along the hems of the garment.
   (iii and iv) Between the main components. The gut strip shown in C(iv) is found along the shoulders and around the base of the sleeves in the places shown thus x−−−−−x.

[2] With all the stitching shown, the outer surface of the garment is towards the top of the drawing.

115. Beechey Collection, Museum no. A.M. 654
   Length, 81 cm. According to the 1836 Ashmolean Museum Catalogue, collected at Kotzebue Sound. (Fig. 73, A-C)

The stitching in shirt number 115 is reinforced by a fine black fibre.

Details concerning Figure 73.
A. & B. Components for the rainshirt.
C.   Stitching used in no.115. The dark reinforcing threads are shaded.
   (i)   Along the hems of the garment.
   (ii) Between the main components.
   (iii) Reinforced stitching from the strip running over the hood and shoulders (a) and over the upper half of the base of the sleeve.

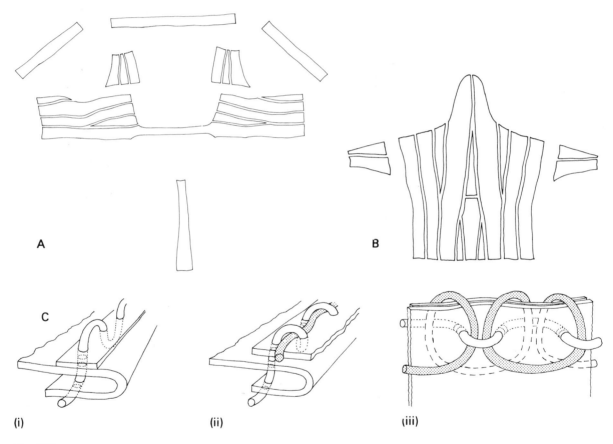

A   B

C

(i)   (ii)   (iii)

Fig. 73

Belt

Dr. John Simpson in the early 1850s reported seeing a belt of caribou teeth—probably similar to Number 116 (Fig. 74)—worn by women at Kotzebue Sound. It was "a piece of skin of proper length having the front teeth of the reindeer adhering to the dried gum of the animal stitched to it, so that the second row of teeth overlies the sewing on the first, and so on, beginning at each end and joining in the middle" (John Simpson, 1854:649). He added that this item was not seen in the Point Barrow area. About twenty-five years later Nelson collected one of these belts and, confirming Simpson's observation, noted that

women wear belts made from the incisors of reindeer taken out with a small fragment of bone, and attached scale-like to a rawhide strap, overlapping each other in a continuous series. When one of these belts has been in the family for a long time, it is believed to acquire a certain virtue for curing disease. In case of rheumatic or other pains the part affected is struck smartly a number of times with the end of the belt and the difficulty is supposed to be relieved (Nelson, 1899:435).

116. Beechey Collection, Museum no. A.M. 665
Length, 68 cm. According to the 1836 Ashmolean Museum Catalogue, collected "N.E. of Icy Cape". (Fig. 74)

A

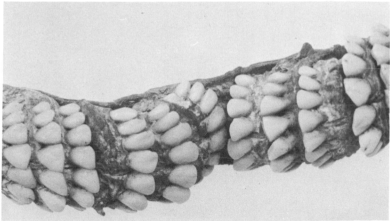

Fig. 74   B

There are seventy-two sets of frontal mandibular caribou teeth attached to the belt and each set has eight teeth, for a total of 576 teeth. The sets are inward-pointing and overlapping, starting at the ends. Thirty-five sets fill one half and thirty-seven are on the other. The size of the sets is graduated from the smallest at the ends to the largest at the centre. They are sewn to a sealskin strip that has a slit at one end.

Sealskin Line

117. Beechey Collection, Museum no. A.M. 690

    Length, about 22 metres; according to Pitt Rivers Museum Catalogue, possibly collected at Port Clarence. (Fig. 75)

The circle of line shown in figure 75 is made of sealskin and carries a label (origin unknown) identifying it as a harpoon line. It is only about 2 mm. by 3 mm. thick, however, and far too thin to have been used on harpoons. Since it is the right size for lashing various objects and is also the size used for the top and bottom lines of fish nets, it may have been meant for either of those purposes. It shows no sign of wear and probably had not been used.

Figs. 75 (left) and 76 (right)

Caribou Sinew Twine

118. Belcher Collection, Museum no. P.R. 1699

    Length, about 10 metres. According to Pitt Rivers Museum Catalogue, collected at Icy Cape. (Fig. 76)

The caribou sinew twine has both three- and four-strand plaiting in it. and could have been used for a variety of tasks.

Walrus tusk

119. Beechey Collection, Museum no. A.M. 684d

    Length, 14.7 cm. According to Pitt Rivers Museum Catalogue, possibly collected at Point Franklin. (Fig. 77)

Fig. 77

A walrus tusk of the size shown in figure 77 must have been taken from a very young animal, possibly a yearling. The tusk may have been kept for use as a raw material.

Artefacts Not Examined

Pitt Rivers Museum

Several artefacts listed in the Pitt Rivers Museum Catalogue were not available when the inventory of the Beechey and Belcher collections was conducted. The catalogue numbers and descriptions are given below for artefacts which probably were collected in northwestern Alaska.

Catalogue Number	*Description*
Beechey Collection	
691	three awls made from bird bones
699	bow drill mouth piece from Kotzebue Sound
715	oval disc of ivory with hole in the centre and a sinew line attached
718	darts
720	dart "with three feathers at butt, for use with spear thrower"
723	bird spear "with triple bone head & barbs along a keeled edge; used with spear thrower"
735	"arrow with bone head notched into 2 barbs; brown-blue stone point; 3 feathers, nocked." Collected "N.E. Icy Cape"
738	"2 arrows lacking stone points, with bone heads keeled & with notched barbs; feathered"
740 and 741	two arrows which have "lost foreshafts and flint heads"
785	sinker-lure
793	"walrus hide harpoon line; 50 yards in one piece"; collected at Port Clarence
Belcher Collection	
Unnumbered	"Shoe grub (ice cleat) of ivory for walking on ice. Western Eskimo"
P.R. 1019	"Bird bolas with 7 stone weights, sinew thread and feathers"
Unnumbered	"Oval bone archer's wrist-guard, with tie thongs through two holes"
P.R. 2129	"Ivory implement with 4 perforations and seal-head carved terminal. Coll. at Icy Cape"
P.R. 2129	"Ivory implement with flat blade with bear-head end and engraved reindeer. Coll. at Icy Cape"
P.R. 2129	"Ivory implement with flat blade and two perforations, bear's head terminal. Coll. at Icy Cape"
P.R. 2126	"Arrow-straightener of ivory carved with heads of bear and young reindeer or musk ox. Coll. at Icy Cape"

P.R. 1959 black	"Eleven pine arrows, nine with bone tops to take stone arrow-heads, one *in situ*, all bearing various owner's marks. Coll. at Icy Cape"
Unnumbered	"Ivory spike with handle, almost central hole, scratched figures of men on side. Coll. at Icy Cape"
Unnumbered	"Ivory implement, lenticular cross-section, tapering to edge, and carved with bear's head handle. Coll. at Icy Cape"
198	"Curved ivory implement, lenticular cross-section, with handle like sword-handle. Coll. at Icy Cape"
Unnumbered	"Long oval ivory implement, lenticular cross-section, carved head on handle, blunt edge. Coll. at Icy Cape"
Unnumbered	"Arrow with 3-barbed bone head. Coll. at Icy Cape"
Unnumbered	"Wooden arrow, butt gone, with obsidian worked point on bone head. Coll. at Icy Cape"

British Museum Specimens

Beechey Collection

A list of Beechey's Eskimo artefacts in the British Museum is presented below in order to allow the reader to judge the breadth of Beechey's Collection. The collection was catalogued at the British Museum in December 1828. Descriptions of the artefacts have been drawn from the Museum's Catalogue.

British Museum Catalogue Number	*Description*
28/12-13/9	"Covering of the head worn by the chief or steersman in the [umiaks].—West Georgia to the N.E. of Icy Cape"
28/12-13/10	"Boots worn by the women at Cape Thompson . . ."
28/13-13/13	"A Skin sail, made from the intestines of the walrus—used in [umiaks] of the natives of Kotzebue Sound"
28/12-13/14	"Man's frock—worn by the natives in Kotzebue Sound"
28/12-13/15	"Woman's frock, worn by the natives at Point Hope"
28/12-13/16	"[ice seive] . . . Kotzebue Sound"
28/12-13/24	"Tooth of the walrus obtained near Point Hope"
28/12-13/25	"Tooth of the walrus obtained from the natives of Point Hope . . ."
28/12-13/27	"Point Barrow—instrument for throwing darts or spears"
28/12-13/29	"Point Barrow—Flint headed spear"
28/12-13/30	"Kotzebue Sound—Flint headed spear"
28/12-13/31	"Point Barrow [dart with throwing board]"
28/12-13/32	"Kotzebue Sound [dart with throwing board]"

28/12-13/34	"Kotzebue Sound—Harpoon"
28/12-13/35	"Harpoon line made from the skin of the walrus—Kotzebue Sound"
28/12-13/37	"7 arrows . . ." (no provenance noted)
28/12-13/38	"2 harpoons with treble barbs" (no provenance noted)
28/12-13/39	"A small spear" (no provenance noted)

Belcher Collection

In 1872 Sir Edward Belcher sold his ethnographic collection; the sale was probably conducted by public auction. Many of the artefacts were purchased by Augustus Wollaston Franks, Keeper of the Department of British and Medieval Antiquities and Ethnography of the British Museum, who donated them to the Museum. The Eskimo artefacts listed below are those which were probably collected during the voyage of H.M.S. *Blossom.*

British Museum Catalogue Number	Description
8192	"Piece of graphite with piece of hide thong passed through it . . . From Point Hope"
8193	"Shoe-shaped piece of graphite tied round with sinew. Point Hope"
8194	"Thin flat slice of graphitic slate used for colouring purposes . . . It requires wetting to make it mark. Point Hope"
8195	"Flat piece of red [haemaetite]? used for painting their paddles, themselves, etc. . . . Point Hope"
8196	"Set of labrets made of walrus ivory, forming a more or less graduated series. . . . Diam. of stem from 1/8 to 3/8 inch"
8197	"Labret of greyish-white stone; semi-spheroidal head; triangular shank. 1 inch by 8/10 in diam. 7/8 inch thick"
8198	"Labret of bright dark-green stone; cylindrical head, ovoid shank. L. 1 1/8 in. W. 1 in."
8199	"Labret made of bright dark-green stone; hemispherical head. . . . L. 1 in."
8200	"Labret made of light-green jade [nephrite], not polished. Discoidal head, oval shank"
8201	"Labret, made of *alabaster*? With a dark-blue glass bead set in the head"
8202	"Labret made of white shell, having a half-oval piece of green stone set into its discoidal head. Oblong shank. D. 1 3/8 in."
8203	"Ivory labret having 3 light-blue spheroidal glass beads affixed to the end of the head . . ."
8204	"Ivory (walrus) labret; cylindrical head having 2 pale-blue and one dark-blue, glass beads fixed at the end"

8205	"Labret, made of mottled lightish-green [nephrite]. L. 3 3/8 in., W. 1 1/4 in., T. 6/10 in."
8206	"Labret, of mottled greenish-grey [nephrite]. L. 3 5/8 in., W. 1 3/8 in., T. 1/2 in."
8207	"Mouth-piece for drilling [bow-drill]. Pine wood, hole at one end, groove along front. Shield-shaped plug of an olive-green stone (nephrite?) . . . L. 5 1/8 in., W. 2 1/8 in."
8208	Bow drill mouth piece, "Wooden . . . ends perforated, tongue at back showing indent marks of teeth of the user. Plug of granite with deep conical cavity to receive end of drill, inserted into the front. L. 4 3/4 in., W. 1 3/4 in."
8209	"Drill bow made of walrus ivory, and engraved on four sides with fishing (whaling etc.) & hunting scenes. Cord of plaited sinew. L. 16 in. W. 3/4 in."
8210	"Drill bow of walrus ivory, ornamented on one side with [a circle-and-dot pattern], and on the other three with hunting, fishing & birding scenes; hide thong. L. over curve 18 inches"
8211	Box handle "of walrus ivory perforated at the ends, ornamented with incised [circle-and-dot pattern] on three sides, & having 5 seals' heads between 4 figures of animals sculptured on the convex side. L. 6 5/8 inches. From neighbourhood of Icy Cape"
8212	"Woman's sewing apparatus [including] *a* Tube of walrus ivory, 4 5/8 inches long, inlaid with pale-blue glass beads; *b* leather thong; *c* ornamented top of another tube having four deep grooves which may serve some practical purpose; *d* . . . a flat ivory hook; *e* a whetstone, light grey striped with blackish, lower end broken off"
8213	"Woman's sewing apparatus [including] a walrus ivory tube, ornamented with engraved [circle-and-dot pattern], through it is passed a hide thong having a European steel needle stuck into it. Attached to lower end of thong are [an awl] 3 7/8 in. long and [two thimble holders], all three of walrus ivory, & a whetstone of bluish-white colour mottled & veined with dark grey. L. 15 3/4 in."
8214	"Polished whetstone of dark-red chert? changing to greenish-grey at the ends, Expanded tang. It belongs to a woman's sewing apparatus. L. 3 1/2 in."
8215	"Needle-shaped [whetstone] of dull milkish-green [nephrite] having an eye at one end. L. 3 7/10 in."
8216	"Needle-like [whetstone] of dark-green [nephrite], pointed end broken off. A groove has been rubbed on one face of the eye end. Hole drilled from both sides. L. 3 4/10 in."
8217	"Thin flat [whetstone] of dull milkish-green [nephrite] having rounded edge and an eye pierced at the broader end. L. 3 in.; W. 6/10 in.; T. 2/10 in."
8218	"Whetstone of light-green jadeite, "flecked with brown. One end is chisel-shaped, bevelled on both faces, the edge dull and rounded; the

other end has a groove rubbed on one side (preparatory to piercing an eye?). L. 4 4/10 in.; W. 4/10 in."

8219	Scraper with grey chert blade and wooden handle; length, 5 1/2 inches
8220	Scraper with grey chert blade and wooden handle; length, 4 3/4 inches; width, 2 5/8 inches. Collected at Icy Cape in 1826
8221	"Bone adze with iron blade 1 5/8 in. wide. The blade is fixed into the bone head & wedged with wood. A slip of wood is placed between the ends of the handle & head which are tied together with hide thongs. Hide thong round handle. L. 14 1/4 inches. Sir Edward obtained this at Point Hope"
8223	Crooked knife made of "a small piece of iron hoop (the projecting part 2 in. long, 1/4 in. wide) inserted into a groove in the edge of one end of a curved bone handle. Binding of split pale [coloured] bark [baleen?]. L. 7 in.; W. 1 1/8 in." Collected at Cape Beaufort
8224	Seal scratcher decoy with "wood handle cut into four digits at the broader end, on which are fixed [seal's] claws secured by sinew cord to an ivory stud fastened to the wood on the concave side of the handle. Transverse hole through butt end. L. 9 5/8 in.; W. 1 7/8 in."
8225	Ulu. "Thin flat iron blade fixed into a grooved handle of walrus ivory . . . Sharp semicircular cutting edge. L. 3 in.; W. 4 1/8 in."
8226	Ulu with green slade blade, shaft made from "Strips of sapling rind" [baleen?]. Length, 5 5/8 inches; width, 3 3/8 inches.
8227	Ulu blade "of dark [coloured] slate, sharpened along the straighter edge, faces smoothed . . . From Point Hope. L. 3 1/4 in.; W. 2 1/2 in.; T. 1/4 in."
8228	Arrow shaft straightener. "A few figures of reindeer and a man shooting at them with bow & arrow, engraved on sides. Walrus head represented on end. Handle end terminating in bear's head. From Point Hope . . . L. 7 3/8 in.; W. 1 5/8 in."
8229	Root pick. "Shoft bulbed wood handle painted red, having a groove at end of bulb into which is fastened a double-pointed curved piece of bone 8 1/2 in. long, 3/4 in. wide, secured with lashings of [baleen]. L. 7 in."
8230	"Scoop-shaped comb made from walrus tusk . . . L. 4 1/8 in.; W. 1 3/8 in." Collected at Cape Beaufort
8232	"Short ivory spoon, having hole in centre of the bowl. Short handle with central cavity, and hole at upper end. Used for eating berries mixed with [seal oil], the superfluous oil escaping by the hole. L. 3 3/4 in.; W. 1 9/16 in." Collected at Chamisso Island
8233	Tool box. "Narrow oblong *box & cover* made of . . . wood, rounded ends, hinges made of two thongs. 4 pale blue glass beads are inlaid in a line along middle of top. End of box mended by a strip of bone being riveted on the edge. L. 9 1/4; W. 2 1/4; H. 2 1/2"
8234	Net gauge of walrus ivory. "L. 9 3/4 in.; W. 1 1/8 in." Collected near Icy Cape

8235	Net gauge of walrus ivory. "Series of [dentate] projections on one side of the handle . . . 8 notches carved on the other. L. 7 3/4 in.; W. 1 1/8 in." Collected near Icy Cape
8236	Burbot and sheefish hook-lure "made of walrus tusk, eyes inlaid, small iron hook with two small yellow claws of a bird attached. Remains of [a baleen] line. Length 5 3/4 inches"
8237	Blubber hook, "wood handle bent at one end which is whipped with whalebone, and sinew cord on account of the splitting; a short ivory hook is fastened at the other. L. 17 inches"
8239	Maul, "oval sectioned head of mottled light-green [nephrite] narrowing off at one end, both showing marks of hammering. Deep groove across one side, and another across narrower end. Bone handle 4 1/2 in. long, slightly grooved at head to receive the hammer, and perforated with hole through which the fastenings pass. The whole of the circumference of the hammer is ground smooth, but no groove is worked to prevent the fastening cords from slipping. Fastening cords of sinew, tightened with a thong; the end of the sinew cord is twisted round the handle end in a closed band. L. 6 3/8 inches." Collected at Point Hope
8240	Part of broken maul head of jadeite. Collected at Cape Beaufort
8241	Flaker "for chipping arrows. Handle made of mammoth ivory, having widely expanded foot, 1 3/4 in. broad, ornamented with incised . . . [circle-and-dot patterns]. Chipper made of reindeer horn. Fastenings of sinew cord. L. 7 in." Collected at Cape Lisburne
8242-43	Waste flakes of grey chert "produced during the manufacture of arrowheads". Collected at Cape Lisburne
8244-45	Unfinished lance blades, No. 8244 collected at Cape Lisburne
8246	Unfinished blade made of chert, probably intended for a lance. "Sir Edward says he took this from the native before he had finished it by forming a tang at bottom." Collected at Cape Lisburne
8247-48	Lance blades made of chert. Collected at Cape Lisburne
8249	Lance blade made of chert
8250-60	Arrow points made of chert
8261-64	Whale harpoon blades made of slate
8265-67	Unfinished walrus harpoon blades of slate
8268	Box for harpoon blades. "Box & cover in form of whale, cut out of . . . wood & the two connected by a cord of plaited sinew, linted with thistle down . . . Blue glass bead inlaid in middle of bottom. L. 7 1/2; W. 3 1/2 in. This box contained seven slate [harpoon blades, probably nos. 8261-67]." Collected at Icy Cape
8269	Whale harpoon head, "made of walrus ivory, slit in top to receive slate blades. The slate [blades, probably nos. 8261-64] belong to it. L. 10 inches." Probably collected at Icy Cape
8273	"Paddle . . . flat blade with remains of red paoint on it; handle neatly

spliced with [baleen] ... L. 4 ft. 7 1/2 in.; W. 6 1/4 in." Collected at Icy Cape

8274   Paddle. "Oval sectioned shaft dying away into the thin flat blade; the latter has 4 ... oblique red stripes painted on the alternate sides of the two faces. L. 5 ft. 2 1/2 in.; W. 5 3/4 in."

8275   "Paddle, ... wood, end of blade & handle stained red ... Eliptical sectional handle grooved along the two sides ... L. 5 ft.; W. 5 3/8 in." Collected between Icy Cape and Point Hope.

Numbers 8222, 8238, 8270, 8271, 8272, 8275 were not included because it was felt that there was some doubt concerning their provenance.

APPENDIX:

Day-to-Day Contact Between the *Blossom*'s Crew and the Eskimos

This appendix is a compendium of information from the journals of the *Blossom*'s officers and men. The ethnographic information contained in the accounts has been extracted and organized in daily entries in order to describe most completely the encounters between the British and the Eskimos. Where there are contradictions between accounts, more than one statement has been presented. In many cases direct quotations have been used in the interest of accuracy. Quotations have been drawn from the accounts of the following: Frederick William Beechey, Captain; George Peard, First Lieutenant; Edward Belcher, Lieutenant; James Wolfe, Admiralty Mate; William Smyth, Admiralty Mate; Thomas Elson, Master; Richard Beechey, Midshipman; and John Bechervaise, Petty Officer.

1826

THE BLOSSOM—*July 17-September 10, 1826*

The sailors first encountered the Eskimos of the Bering Strait region at Saint Lawrence Island. The natives there are closely related to the Eskimos of the Chukotsk Peninsula and speak a dialect that is unintelligible to the inhabitants of northwestern Alaska.

July 17, 1826: at a small bay on the southwestern corner of Saint Lawrence Island.

The ship was approached by four umiaks with eight people, both male and female, in each. They offered to trade nets, walrus ivory, skin shirts, harpoons, bows and arrows, small birds and skins (Beechey, 1831:I, 243-44), and they displayed a knowledge of trading practices. (Plate III).

James Wolfe recorded the encounter:
> On coming up with the Ship, they did not appear the least alarmed, and from the number of articles with them it was evident they were come for the purpose of bartering.
> The first word they uttered was 'tobacco' . . . but they would only take that weed in the leaf.
> The women seemed only to wish for beads, the blue color being most prised, yellow they would not have. From their making it a rule to bite them we conceived that they had been duped with compositions of wax.
> They appeared to have no wish to come board the Ship but remained quietly alongside; the four boats occupied the whole length of the vessel . . . the ship's side was lined with officers and men holding out tobacco, beads, buttons or whatever was thought likely to be acceptable exhibiting a variety of passions & feelings in their anxiety to procure the trinkets of these people, exceeding perhaps their eagerness for our wares. (Wolfe, n.d.:110-111)

July 21, 1826: at Shishmaref Inlet

Two umiaks with nine people in each came to the ship to barter (Wolfe, n.d.:111).[1]

At Shishmaref Inlet Beechey described the trading and noticed "a considerable village of yourts" after having seen "several Esquimaux habitations" between there and Cape Prince of

---

[1] Wolfe recorded the place of trade as near Cape Espenberg. This was the only trade encounter noted for the day in any of the journals, and Beechey's location of the event at Shishmaref Inlet is probably more to be trusted (Beechey, 1831:I, 247).

Wales. "'They willingly sold everything they had," he said, "except their bows and arrows, which they implied were required for the chase on shore; but they could not resist 'tawac' (tobacco) and iron knives, and ultimately parted with them" (Beechey, 1831:I, 247-48).

Beechey remarked that the Eskimos' rain shirts were "on the whole as good as the best oil-skins in England", and he added that "to the end of that which goes around the waist they attach a tuft of hair, the wing of a bird, or sometimes a fox's tail, which ... may probably have occasioned the report of the Tschutschi, recorded in Muller [Jeffreys, 1761], that the people of the country have 'tails like dogs' " (Beechey, 1831:I, 248-49). At Shismaref Inlet he also bought a labret that was 3 inches long and 1½ inches wide. This must have been similar to the one sketched by Belcher (Plate VII).

July 22, 1826: off the mouth of Hotham Inlet.[2]

As far as can be determined, seven umiaks arrived for trading, and according to Richard Beechey (n.d.:41), there were six to ten men in each boat (Plate IX). Captain Beechey (1831:I, 250), however, estimated ten to thirteen persons per boat. The first boat sold dried salmon and a "sort of caplin," but the next six arrived and offered skins that "were far superior to any before seen even at Kamschatka"; there were polar bear, caribou, ermine, white and red fox, muskrat and bird skins. Drill bows were also offered (Wolfe, n.d.:113-14).

Belcher's account varied slightly from the other descriptions. Six umiaks, he said,

> having from 9 to 11 men and women in each pulled off, but the Capt. motioning them to go (as we were busily employed) it was not without difficulty that we afterwards by waving persuaded them to return, making use of their friendly gestures, which consist in raising both hands (describing a semicircle with the arm as radius) above the head then bringing them down to the chest and patting it which is repeated several times and considered an act of friendly salutation. Salmon, dried cod and caplin besides weapons and ornaments were the chief articles trafficked for, in exchange for which they took blue beads, tobacco, knives & pewter rings, but the beads certainly had the preference. (Belcher, n.d.:29)

Between July 23 and July 30, 1826: near Hotham Inlet.

The barge joined the *Blossom* at Chamisso Island on July 30. Its crew reported "that a very large river ran up there and having met with many [umiaks] had purchased numerous weapons &c for Govt." (Belcher, n.d.:30).

August 1, 1826: north of Cape Krusenstern (near 67°55′N).[3]

Three umiaks paddled at least ten miles to reach the ship and to trade for beads, knives and tobacco (Beechey, 1831:I, 262; Wolfe, n.d.:117).

August 2, 1826: at Cape Thompson

A party from the ship landed to set up a signal post for Franklin and found there was a "small encampment at the stream" consisting of eight tents and fifteen people.[4] When the Eskimos came forward to barter (Plate X), they laid down their arms and "eagerly sought an exchange of goods." Their arms, according to Beechey, were iron-headed spears; and Wolfe

---

[2]Wolfe's account (n.d.:113) seems to place this encounter nearer Cape Krusenstern, but again Beechey's location seems more reliable, and the meeting probably occurred off Sheshalik, where the natives met annually for a trade fair.

[3]Peard (1973:152) gives this latitude.

[4]The number of people per tent seems quite low. Foote (1965:225) estimated an average of about seven persons per tent.

Plate IX Lithograph of Baidars of Hotham Inlet from Beechey's "Journal of a Voyage . . ."

Plate X Lithograph of natives trading at Cape Thompson from Beechey's "Journal of a Voyage . . ."

noted that they were frightened by a shotgun, which led him to believe they had never seen a firearm before (Beechey, 1831:I, 262-63; Wolfe, n.d.:118-19).

"Very few of their tribe understood better how to drive a bargain than these people; and it was not until they had sold almost all they could spare, that we had any peace" wrote Beechey (1831:I, 262). Wolfe's journal (n.d.:118) notes that "Finding us purchase so many little trinkets which to them were worthless, they at last began to pick up dried fish & birds bones, stones etc and offer them for beads & tobacco; and appeared to hold our common sense very cheap."

August 3, 1826: at Point Hope.

At Point Hope one umiak visited the ship, but the crew found the village largely deserted except for children and old people (Beechey, 1831:I, 266-69; Peard, 1973:152). Belcher (n.d.:33) recorded that they were able to buy a few bows and some fishing gear. Richard Beechey (n.d.:56) noted that there were thirty or forty houses "in pretty good repair", but there were not more than twelve people left in the village.[5] The rest of the inhabitants were, no doubt, away on summer trading voyages or were on hunting and fishing trips (Rainey, 1947).

August 7, 1826: at Cape Lisburne.

One umiak came to the ship to trade (Richard Beechey, n.d.:56). (Plate XI).

Plate XI Detail of a sketch of an umiak at Cape Lisburne with the barge in the distance. August 7th 1826. Reproduced with the sanction of Controller of H.M.S.O. and the Hydrographer of the Navy.

August 8, 1826: northeast of Cape Lisburne, possibly at Cape Beaufort.

Two umiaks visited the ship with the carcasses of three young walrus in the boats. Some of the ship's crew, who had been with Parry in the eastern Arctic, bought walrus meat (Wolfe, n.d.:121).

August 14, 1826: a short distance north of Icy Cape, possibly at Killimitavik.

Two houses were seen "at the entrance to a lake" (Beechey, 1831:I, 272). Twenty-five

[5] Richard Beechey gave the date as August 5.

quarters of caribou weighing four hundred pounds were bought for four pounds of tobacco (Peard, 1973:154).[6] Beechey added that they bought two swans and that

> These swans were without their feet, which had been converted into bags, after the practice of the eastern Esquimaux; and it is remarkable, that although so far from Kamtschatka and the usual track of vessels, these people expressed no surprise at the appearance either of the ship or of the boat, and that they were provided both with knives and iron kettles. (Beechey, 1831:I, 272)

Perhaps the Eskimos were not excited at the arrival of the British, because Russian ships had been in the area five years before.

The Eskimos also ferried the sailors across the lagoon in their umiaks (Peard, 1973:154).

August 15, 1826: at Point Franklin.

In the winter of 1884-85 Charles Brower (n.d.) travelled along the coast from Cape Lisburne to Point Barrow and reported that six families were living at the tip of Point Franklin (Pingasugaruk), that twelve houses were occupied at Point Belcher (Sidaru) and that the village of Atanik had been abandoned. Beechey seems to be referring to the latter village in this passage:

> The natives taking advantage of this elevated ground had constructed their winter residences in it; they were very numerous, and extended some way along the coast. The season, however, was not yet arrived at which the Esquimaux take up their abode in their subterranean habitations, and they occupied skin tents upon a low point at the entrance of the lake. We had not been long off here before three [umiaks] from the village paddled alongside and bartered their articles as usual. Some of the crew ascended the side of the ship without any invitation, and showed not the least surprise at any thing they beheld; which I could not help particularly remarking, as we were not conscious of any other vessel having been upon the coast since Kotzebue's voyage, and he did not reach within two hundred miles of the residence of these people. (Beechey, 1831:I, 273-74)

Belcher reported similar observations:

> Three of the [umiaks] from the nearest village visited us ... but far from appearing surprised at the sight of a ship, they on the contrary began immediately to make signs for Tobacco & knives, & a traffic was speedily commenced. These people brought some of the largest teeth (of walrus) that we had yet seen. (Belcher, n.d.:40)[7]

The village Beechey and Belcher referred to is possibly where Bechervaise obtained his baleen fish net (page 52) and reported another interesting encounter. Sailors came upon a group of about thirty tents, he said, one of which was smaller than the rest and occupied by an old, white-haired woman:

> Her appearance seemed to indicate approaching dissolution; before her was placed a small trough in which blubber cut in small square pieces had been thrown; the hut was barely large enough for her to sit upright in. It was the general opinion that when these people became old and useless or incapable of looking out for themselves, they are thus fed at common charge, for this was the third hut we had observed thus tenanted. ([Bechervaise], 1839:207)

August 17, 1826: at Blossom Shoals.

The Captain ordered the barge, which had been sailing in company with the ship, to proceed alone to the north in search of Franklin's party.

---

[6] Beechey (1831:I, 272) agreed with Peard on the amount of caribou. Wolfe, however, stated that eighteen quarters, weighing 328 pounds were purchased (n.d.:124).

[7] Belcher recorded the date as August 16.

August 20, 1826: near Cape Beaufort.

In Beechey's narrative for this date he stated that his party had no sooner stepped ashore than an umiak full of people landed a short distance away. The crew of the umiak

consisted of three grown-up males and four females, besides two infants. They were as ready as their neighbours to part with what they had in exchange for trifles; esteeming our old brass buttons above all other articles, excepting knives. There was a blear-eyed old hag of the party, who separated from her companions, and seated herself upon a piece of driftwood at a little distance from the [umiak], and continued there muttering in an unintelligible language and apparently believing herself to be holding communion with that invisible world to which she was fast approaching. Though in her dotage, her opinion was often consulted, and on more than one occasion in a mysterious manner. We afterwards witnessed several instances of extremely old women exercising great influence over the younger part of the community. (Beechey, 1831:I, 279-80)

Richard Beechey (n.d.:71) wrote that he was informed that the Eskimos' umiak was drawn along shore by five dogs.

August 26, 1826: at Point Hope.

Richard Beechey recorded that Wainwright and Smyth went ashore and that they saw the same Eskimos they had met there earlier in the month.

They had neither bow, arrow, spear or in fact any thing whatever with them, but on embarking Mr. Wolfe made a present to each of the females of a string of beads. This favor being excluded from the males was not at all understood. Mr. Wolfe acknowledges the favors of one of the ladies charms, who was dressed in a salmons skin gown, and whose appearance had before won the heart of one of our brother officers. (Richard Beechey, n.d.:72)

August 28, 1826: at Chamisso Island.

When the *Blossom* reached Chamisso it was found that a barrel of flour, which the sailors had buried there for Franklin earlier in the summer, had been dug up and the iron hoops taken from it. Beechey (1831:I, 283-84), assumed this had been done by a group of Eskimos camped nearby. Peard noticed six umiaks and some tents on the beach at the south end of Choris Peninsula (Peard, 1973:157).

August 29, 1826: on Choris Peninsula.

On the day following the discovery of the damaged cask Beechey landed on Choris Peninsula and visited some Eskimos he had met the day before. He wrote that the natives walked down to meet them

with their arms drawn in from their sleeves, and tucked up inside their frocks. They were also very particular that every one of them should salute us, which they did by licking their hands, and drawing them first over their own faces and bodies, and then over ours . . . but they would on no account suffer us to approach their tents; and, when we urged it, seemed determined to resist, even with their weapons, which were carefully laid out upon a low piece of ground near them. They were resolved, nevertheless, that we should partake of their hospitality, and seating us upon a rising ground, placed before us strips of blubber in wooden bowls, and whortle berries mashed up with fat and oil, or some such heterogeneous substance, for we did not taste it. Seeing we would not partake of their fare, they commenced a brisk traffic with dried salmon, of which we procured a great quantity. Generally speaking, they were honest in their dealings, leaving their goods with us, when they were in doubt about a bargain, until they had referred it to a second person, or more commonly to some of the old women. If they approved of it, our offer was accepted; if not, they took back their goods. On several occasions, however, they tried to impose upon us with fish-skins, ingeniously put together to represent a whole fish, though entirely deprived of their original contents: but this artifice succeeded only once: the natives, when detected in other attempts, laughed heartily, and treated the affair as a fair practical joke. (Beechey, 1831:I, 285)

Beechey found that the natives also tried to convince him through sign language that another group had damaged the cask of flour and then had departed with the hoops. This information he discounted because, among other reasons, he assumed this group had been concealing the flour in their tents and would, therefore, not allow him to approach them. (Beechey, 1831:I, 285-86)

August 30, 1826: at Chamisso Island.

As the group of Eskimos on Choris Peninsula was leaving the area it was reported to Captain Beechey that other Eskimos who "differed in several particulars from those upon the peninsula" were camped on nearby Chamisso Island. Like the others, these Eskimos were on their way to their winter homes with a large store of food. Their camp consisted of four tents and several umiaks, and they were suspected of having been involved in damaging the flour cask because some flour was seen in their camp (Beechey, 1831:I, 286). It was also reported to Beechey that the women of the group differed from other women they had seen in that they had

> the septum of the nose pierced, and a large blue bead strung upon a strip of [baleen] passed through the orifice, the bead hanging as low as the opening of the mouth. One of them, on receiving a large stocking-needle, thrust it into the orifice, or, as some of the seamen said, 'spritsail-yarded her nose.' A youth of the party who had not yet had his lips perforated wore his hair in bunches on each side of the head after the fashion of the women, which I notice as being the only instance of the kind we met with. (Beechey, 1831:I, 286-87)

The crew purchased 150 pounds of dried salmon from this group (Peard, 1973:157), and the British trade goods included red and blue beads, hatchets, knives, buttons, and a mirror, the latter of which caused great excitement among the Eskimos (Beechey, 1831:I, 287). In the evening the Eskimos broke camp and left before further contact was made with them (Beechey, 1831:I, 286).

August 30–September 2, 1826: on Choris Peninsula.

On August 30 Captain Beechey, after being told of the Eskimo group at Chamisso Island, went again to visit the party encamped on Choris Peninsula. The Eskimos there, he learned, were on their way to their home at Cape Prince of Wales. He counted twenty-five people in the group, five tents and seven umiaks (Beechey, 1831:I, 290-91).[8] On arrival at their camp he was greeted warmly, but as on August 29 (p. 109), he was not allowed to approach their tents. The natives locked arms with the British and led them to an area of higher ground, where the sailors were seated on planks and skins. Each was presented with a dried fish, and then offered a bowl containing a mixture of berries, greens and fat, which the British declined. After that, the Eskimos prepared for dancing by appearing in their best clothes—which they were unwilling to sell to the sailors until the dance was finished—and seated themselves in two concentric circles with the Eskimo men composing the inner one and the Eskimo women and children the outer circle. Beechey reported that

> in addition to their usual costume, some had a kind of tippet of ermine and sable skins thrown over their

---

[8] Wolfe, however, recorded that there were forty natives from Cape Prince of Wales. The group was composed of five families, each with an umiak and a tent (Wolfe, n.d.*a*:83, 131-32).

shoulders, and others wore a band on their heads, with strips of skin suspended to it at every two inches, to the end of which were attached the nails of seals. (Beechey, 1831:I, 289)

After the dancing had ended, the two groups began bartering, and Beechey mentioned that a mirror caused great excitement among the Eskimos, to the extent that they held it before the face of a blind man. Other trade items were hatchets, knives, and red and blue beads (Beechey, 1831:I, 287-89). Among other things, the British bought 172 pounds of dried fish (Wolfe, n.d.:131-32). During the trading, the Eskimos attempted to pilfer from the British, but when they were detected, the particular item was returned with "a hearty laugh". One of them cut a button from the tail of the Captain's coat, but returned it when discovered (Wolfe, n.d.*a*: 76).

Wolfe observed that these people were competent traders:

From the somewhat superior intelligence displayed by this party, we concluded that they were more in the habit of intercourse with other people than any we had before seen. They understood two or three of the Kamtschadale words and appeared perfectly aware of the value of several articles offered in barter; of which however blue beads were in highest estimation. (Wolfe, n.d.*a*:75-76)

Beechey also detected a difference in pronunciation between this group and others he had visited. The Eskimos would not allow the British to write in their notebooks during the visit, however, and the Captain was unable to document this variation (Beechey, 1831:I, 293).

The Eskimos showed that they were well acquainted with the trade in iron for they tested the British knives and hatchets "by hacking at them with their own. If they stood the blow they were accepted, but if, on the contrary, they were notched, they were refused" (Beechey, 1831:I, 289). The Eskimo women wore broad iron bracelets such as the officers had not seen before, and "by their having four or five of them upon each wrist, it appeared that this metal, so precious with the tribes to the northward, was with them less rare" (Beechey, 1831:I, 293).

Wolfe said that

some small hatchets, which in that shape had been but little prized, were by the armourer converted into adzes, and for these they would have given anything. They hugged them and showed the greatest eagerness to possess them. This was a great point gained, and as the captain wished to purchase a baydair (Kaiyak or Oomiak) he offered two for a new one. They would readily have consented but signified that they should not have enough left to carry their party. (Wolfe, n.d.*a*:82)

During his visit to the *Blossom*, the native leader had demonstrated by his actions that his previous contacts with Europeans, if any, had been limited. He marvelled at the workmanship of the vessel, but Beechey found that "he seemed to regret that so much iron had been expended where thongs would have served as well". The Eskimo also was amazed at the weight of the sounding lead used to test the depth of the water (Beechey, 1831:I, 292).

The Eskimos one day drew a map in the sand for Beechey. He found it to be an accurate representation of the coast from Cape Krusenstern to Cape Darby. Of particular interest to the Captain was their delineation of Port Clarence, a place Beechey claimed not to have known about. As the Eskimos were leaving, their leader suggested that the British should also leave, but Beechey made it understood that his party would stay nearly three weeks longer. The Eskimos by sign language then warned that the weather would soon turn very cold (Beechey, 1831:I, 291-92).

As they left, the Eskimos made warm gestures of friendship to the British. Shortly thereafter, traces of flour were discovered in their campsite, which suggested that as Beechey had suspected on August 29, they had been party to the damaging of the flour cask (Beechey, 1831:I, 292-93).

September 3, 1826: at Chamisso Island.

Another umiak in the long procession of boats returning to winter quarters arrived at the ship on September 3. Peard (1973:158) recorded that the Eskimos were not very interested in tobacco, and Richard Beechey was informed that they showed fear of the British (Richard Beechey, n.d.:92).

September 6, 1826: at Chamisso Island.

Two umiaks carrying two families arrived under sail.[9] From a distance, through the fog, the British thought the boats might be those of Franklin's party because the sails did not seem similar to the Eskimo type but seemed to be lug-rigged (Beechey, 1831:I, 294; Richard Beechey, n.d.:92). Each group was carrying its own equipment, and from their language, the Captain assumed they were from Cape Prince of Wales. He found them to be more friendly and open in their manner than the group they had earlier met from there. The British bought from them about one hundred pounds of dried fish as well as some bows and other goods (Richard Beechey, n.d.:92). The Captain was fascinated by the amount of cargo carried in the umiaks:

> From two of these they landed fourteen persons, eight tent poles, forty deer skins, two kyacks, many hundredweight of fish, numerous skins of oil, earthen jars for cooking, two living foxes, ten large dogs, bundles of lances, harpoons, bows, and arrows, a quantity of [baleen], skins full of clothing, some immense nets made of hide for taking small whales and porpoises, eight broad planks, masts, sails, paddles, &c., besides [walrus] hides and teeth, and a variety of nameless articles always to be found among the Esquimaux. (Beechey, 1831:I, 295)

Although this group appeared to be poorer than the previous one from Cape Prince of Wales, they were well supplied with foreign trade goods (Beechey, 1831:I, 295; Richard Beechey, n.d.:92). Wolfe (n.d.:136) noted that the natives made fire with iron and pyrites. The women wore beads hanging from their ears and attached to their clothing, and—to the surprise of the British—some of the women had bells sewed under their parkas:

> When they moved, several bells were set ringing, and on examining their persons, we discovered that they had each three or four of these instruments under their clothes, suspended to their waists, hips, and one even lower down. (Beechey, 1831:I, 295)

Later Beechey was shown both a Russian coin imprinted with the head of Empress Catherine and a halberd head that had been converted to a knife.

Trade was carried on, and the Eskimos were paid with "necklaces of blue beads, brooches and cutlery" (Beechey, 1831:I, 297). The *Blossom* took on about one hundred pounds of fish. This group of Eskimos did not object to Beechey's writing and drawing in his notebook. As a result, he was able to make notes on their vocabulary and to draw a few sketches of the people.

September 7, 1826: at Chamisso Island.

On this day, after the natives had paid a visit to the ship, Richard Beechey and Charles Osmer went ashore to buy some skins. Richard Beechey (n.d.:92) noted that the Eskimos showed "surprize at my knocking off a small wooden bowl from the top of a post with my gun, particularly when they afterwards found it pierced with shot."

September 8, 1826: at Chamisso Island.

Captain Beechey returned to the Eskimo camp and found that the price of the articles they offered for sale had risen severalfold (Beechey, 1831:I, 300).

---

[9] Peard gives the date as September 1 (1973:158).

September 10, 1826: at Chamisso Island.

The barge ended its voyage of discovery by rejoining the *Blossom* at Chamisso Island. The Captain was told of its itinerary and of the crew's adventures. A compendium of the accounts follows.

THE BARGE—*August 17—September 10, 1826*

On August 17, 1826, at Blossom Shoals Captain Beechey ordered the barge, which had been sailing with the *Blossom*, to proceed north along the coast in search of Franklin's party. Beechey then returned south in the *Blossom* to carry out other surveys. The barge was commanded by Thomas Elson, Master, with William Smyth, Admiralty Mate, second in command. They had a crew of six seamen and two marines (Beechey, 1831:I, 278).

August 18, 1826: near Icy Cape.

In the morning, when the barge was south of Icy Cape, an umiak with seven people came to it, and they "exchanged some trifles" with the sailors. At noon the barge was near Icy Cape and some dwellings were noticed on shore (Elson, 1973:159). This was probably the settlement of Kayaakseravik which was recorded by Spencer (1959:8) and Stefansson (1909:601-10) as having been located there.
In 1838 A.F. Kaschevarof met 300 Eskimos there (VanStone:n.d.).

August 19, 1826: north of Icy Cape.

The barge reached a deserted village, probably Mitliktavik, north of Icy Cape, and Smyth investigated one of the houses. His description of it follows (see also pp. 123-125):
> The ground is excavated to a depth of 4 feet which is nearly half the height of the apartment. The ground floor was two feet above the earth, and from the floor to the roof is 5 feet 10 inches high in the centre, and the eaves only 4 feet. The hut was 12 feet long and 8 broad. One side is divided in two horizontally by a flooring 3 feet above the first, on or under which we supposed they slept. In the ground floor was a hole a foot and a half in diameter which leads to an underground passage, hardly large enough to crawl through on hands and knees. This passage was 8 or 10 feet and led out through an entrance, well protected from the weather by another passage 15 to 20 feet long, constructed of logs, and high enough to admit walking upright under. These passages appeared to be the winter entry into the hut. (Smyth, n.d.*a*:112)

Later, moving north, the barge encountered sixty people in four umiaks. This may have been in the vicinity of the village of Killimitavik. The crew tried to barter for caribou meat, but the natives would not go ashore for it (Elson, 1973:159); instead the sailors only brought "a few of their trinkets" and went on (Smyth, n.d.*a*:113).

August 20, 1826: near Wainwright Inlet.

On the 20th, the barge and its crew passed close to the village of Oroonek (Stefansson, 1909:601-10) near Wainwright Inlet and met four umiaks with forty people. The crew landed sixteen miles farther along the coast to take observations and, three miles beyond, met two Eskimos (Elson, 1973:160; Wolfe, n.d.*a*:137). Later, at the village of Sidaru on Point Belcher, several dwellings were seen. After that some umiaks were encountered and meat was purchased (Elson, 1973:160).

August 21, 1826: near Point Franklin.

On the way to Point Franklin several umiaks were met, possibly near the village of Atanik, and one of the umiaks was bought for two hatchets (Smyth, 1831:306). Elson recorded an encounter where several umiaks came alongside the barge

> and one of the Natives cut a piece out of the clue of the Foretopsail . . . Sent them all away. They continued to follow us, but were not allowed alongside. On a former Occasion, they managed to take from the deck, unperceived, a Black Jack & Carpenter's plane; on being discovered, they soon delivered them up. (Elson, 1973:160)

Smyth (n.d.*a*:114; n.d.*b*:138) recorded that they passed a deserted tent village; this was most probably Pingasugaruk.

August 22, 1826: near Point Barrow.

Passing northward along the coast, the sailors saw several tent camps. They met an umiak with three women in it and bartered for furs and caribou meat, then passed the village of Walakpa at Refuge Inlet. They saw other villages, probably Utkeavik (Barrow) and Piginek (Birnirk), as they continued up the coast (Elson, 1973:160-61; Smyth, n.d.*a*:115).

August 23, 1826: at Point Barrow.

At about 2.00 A.M. the barge reached Point Barrow, the northernmost point in Alaska, and Elson tentatively named the Point "World's End", because he could see no land to the East, West or North. The sailors found the village there, Nuwuk, to be the largest they had seen. At first, two umiaks came off to them and their passengers seemed unsure whether they should approach the vessel (Plate XII). They were given some tobacco and beads, and, after they had returned to shore, other groups visited the barge. Smyth noted that their bows differed from

Plate XII Lithograph of Point Barrow by William Smyth from Beechey's "Journal of a Voyage . . ."

Plate XIV Watercolour of the barge leaving Point Barrow, August 23rd, 1826, by William Smyth. Courtesy of Elmer E. Rasmuson.

others he had seen in that the tension cables were "strengthened" with baleen. He also recorded that many of the men wore oblong labrets about three inches long by one inch wide (Smyth, 1831:I, 308). The sailors purchased some artefacts, but the Eskimos began to try to steal from them, and contact was broken off. The aggressive behaviour of the Eskimos forced the British to conclude that it would be unsafe for them to go ashore to leave a message for Franklin (Elson, 1973:161-62; Smyth, 1831:I, 308). In 1838 Kashevarof's party also encountered hostile natives there (VanStone, n.d.).

The barge was then taken more than a mile northwest of the point for observations, and on its return near shore it was met by about twenty natives armed with bows, arrows and spears. Smyth noted that the Eskimos thought the English wished to land, and

> they made signs for us to remain on board. They appeared quite prepared for hostilities, some of them nearly naked and, preserving a more than ordinary silence, but one spoke at a time, seemingly interrogating us with regard to our intentions. The natives kept walking abreast to us. (Smyth, n.d.*a*:118). (Plate XIV).
>
> The barge then continued south along shore, and about 8 PM we passed a village [probably Piginek] of 8 tents and 4 boats but saw neither women nor children: previous to our reaching this place we perceived them hauling their [umiaks] higher up. About 11 our friends having tired of the chase stopped and after watching us for some time longer, returned. (Smyth, n.d.*a*:118)

August 24, 1826: near Refuge Inlet.

The ice closed in on the barge and the crew was forced to tow it from shore by means of a track line. When they arrived at Refuge Inlet, they found nine tents at the village of Walakpa (Smyth, n.d.*b*:141). They established friendly relations with the natives there, first by throwing some presents ashore, and then by distributing leaves of tobacco. The Eskimos helped with the track line, but the current running into the inlet was too strong to allow them to pass easily, and once on the other side, the boat grounded, and the ice completely closed in (Smyth, 1831:I, 311-14).

August 25, 1826: at Refuge Inlet.

It was probably after this that Smyth was able to examine some of the tents in the camp:[10]

> The tents were constructed [of] a few sticks placed in the ground and meeting at the top so as to give the dwelling when covered with hides a conical form, in these however being intended for a greater degree of cold a lining of Reindeer skins was suspended. A few logs formed the floor on which were spread the skins for sleeping. They cooked their provisions in open air in earthen pots, putting in blood entrails blubber & flesh all together: their chief food is the Walrus Seal Reindeer & Fish and procuring more in the summer than sufficient for present use, the other is buried in the sand for winter consumption. They very kindly dug up a seal which had evidently been deposited for some time, and one of them put his hand into the intestines, stirred them up and offered us a handful to eat. The sight of it was enough to turn the stomach even of Captain Cook. (Smyth, n.d.*b*:142)

One old man who visited the barge, after having been given a present of beads and tobacco, "offered up what [they] concluded to be a prayer, at the same time blowing with his mouth, as if imploring an east wind and the dispersion of the ice.—In the afternoon the wind had increased to a gale" (Smyth, 1831:I, 314).

---

[10]Both Captain Beechey and Richard Beechey, quoting Smyth (1831:I, 315; n.d.*a*:125) recorded that this visit occurred on August 25; however Wolfe's quotation from Smyth's journal (n.d.*b*:142) gives the date as August 24.

August 27, 1826: at Refuge Inlet.

The ice remained packed on shore, and the sailors, worried that they would be trapped for the winter, began cutting a track for the barge. Some Eskimos assisted without having been asked to do so (Smyth, 1831:I, 316).

September 5, 1826: near Cape Lisburne.

While a party was ashore getting wood and water, a native stole some tobacco and beads from the pocket of one of the sailors and ran away. Two musket shots were fired over his head (Elson, 1973:166).[11] Later, an umiak from Cape Lisburne, carrying eleven people, visited the vessel (Elson, 1973:166).

September 6, 1826: from Cape Lisburne to Point Hope.

South of Cape Lisburne, probably at Cape Dyer, five umiaks and one tent were noticed (Smyth, n.d.*a*:126; n.d.*b*.:144). In the evening, the barge, in heavy seas, passed Point Hope, and the houses on shore were visible (Elson, 1973:167).

September 8, 1826: near Cape Krusenstern.

Near Cape Krusenstern the barge was visited by "several" Eskimos, and some fish was purchased from them (Elson, 1973:167).

September 9, 1826: at Sheshalik.

Approaching Sheshalik, Elson wrote that the natives "continued to pester" them; however, when they reached shore, they found that no tents remained (1973:167). The people who had been attending the trade fair there had already dispersed.

September 10, 1826: at Chamisso Island.

The barge reached the *Blossom* at 1.30 PM (Elson, 1973:167) and thus completed an important voyage of discovery. In addition to the geographical knowledge that was acquired, a significant amount of ethnographical information had been collected.

September 10, 1826: near Elephant Point.

The barge was almost immediately sent on a short exploratory trip, and on returning from the mouth of the Buckland River the sailors were met by seven kayaks. The natives were "very troublesome, pestering [the British for tobacco and receiving it] in the most ungracious manner, without offering any in return" (Beechey, 1831:I, 322-23). Beechey watched an Eskimo from the Buckland River area demonstrate the use of a bird dart (Beechey, 1831:I, 324).

[11]Captain Beechey and Peard, quoting Smyth (1831:I, 319) and Elson (1973:166) respectively, recorded this incident as having occurred on September 5. Richard Beechey's quotation from Smyth lists the date as September 4 (Smyth, n.d.*a*.:125).

The BLOSSOM—*September 11-October 10, 1826*

September 11, 1826: at Chamisso Island.

An umiak visited the ship and sold some fish, and one of the natives tried to steal a compass from a boat (Peard, 1973:168; Richard Beechey, n.d.:95).[12]

September 20, 1826: at Chamisso Island.

Wolfe, the Admiralty Mate, was sent ashore at Chamisso to take observations, and on landing found a group of ten men and one old woman. He ordered his crew to talk with the natives and keep them distracted so that he could take his observations without interference. He was not entirely successful, as his journal shows:

> The brass shining so bright, and the novelty of the appearance, excited a strong desire to see them closer, but on the boat's crew signifying that they must not, they appeared to acquiesce tho reluctantly with the exception of the old hag . . . who was no so complaisant; she seemed to insist on approaching, and as the men did not like to use force, had already gained the place where I was & was about to take hold of some of the instruments when I called some of our crew to carry her away. The male relatives during this time had remained quiet spectators, but on the female being thus repulsed she motioned them to retire and then in the most formal manner commenced imprecations against us and those most heartily. She bent her body putting her hands on her knees, and in this position kept up for about five minutes a croaking noise like a toad looking all the time steadily at us with a scowl on her countenance, then muttering some words, held up her hands toward the sun, repeatedly changing them toward us: after this she croaked at us again & retired. Some of the boat's crew followed her to her companions and observed them all prostrate on the ground, evidently engaged in some superstitious (or what is nearly synonymous) religious ceremonies using many gesticulations with their hands, apparently addressing the Sun—This is the only instance I have witnessed of anything like worship good or evil or of their holding any object in religious awe or veneration—Having completed the observations, I was about to return on board when I perceived the party advancing making the usual signs of friendship which were returned and the old woman was amongst the first to offer us some berries. A few things were purchased tho' they were such a miserable set that they did not seem to have werewithal for their own use. At last they became troublesome and very importunate for blue beads; a [loon] happening to light near the boat I offered a string of beads if they would shoot it, they soon got into the [umiak] and paddled along very quietly, when within about 20 yards the man in the bow let fly two arrows in astonishingly quick succession one of which pierced the bird thro' both eyes. So smartly did one arrow follow the other, that I am sure the man had not time to notice whether the first was effective or not. I therefore conclude it must be a practise among them, in order to make more sure of their prey, and the arrows can easily be recovered. From the dexterity with which this feat was performed, I must recant from the generality of a former remark and call to mind a hint of Dean Swift's in Gulliver's voyage to Lilliput, to be careful in pronouncing an opinion or of drawing too hasty a conclusion of the habits, manners &c of natives with whom we have had an imperfect acquaintance. (Wolfe, n.d.:146)[13]

September 23, 1826: on Baldwin Peninsula.

Richard Beechey and Thomas Elson, on foot, crossed to the east side of Baldwin Peninsula about six miles south of Cape Blossom and discovered Hotham Inlet. Elson bought some fresh salmon there from a group of Eskimos going south in an umiak. The natives had two swans and a large number of ptarmigan (Richard Beechey, n.d.:99).

[12]Richard Beechey gives the date as September 12.

[13]Peard (1973:169), who did not witness the shooting of the loon, gives the date as September 23 and the distance as forty yards.

September 25, 1826: near Cape Blossom.

Some Eskimos were seen putting out seal nets, and the British bought about two bushels of "whortle berries" from them (Beechey, 1831:I, 330).

September 26, 1826: near Cape Blossom.

Fresh salmon and trout were purchased from Eskimos in an umiak. "The coxswain of this boat wore unusually large labrets, consisting of blue glass beads fixed upon circular pieces of ivory a full inch in diameter". The Eskimo drew a map of Hotham Inlet in the sand for the British (Beechey, 1831:I, 330-31).

October 1, 1826: at Sheshalik.

Beechey landed at Sheshalik in the barge while trying to find a channel into Hotham Inlet. He had met the natives there several months before, and this time he traded beads with them for fresh salmon, herring and some nets (Beechey, 1831:I, 331-32; Peard, 1973:170). Beechey noted that

> the people whom we saw here were very inquisitive about our fire-arms, and to satisfy one of them I made him fire off a musket, that was loaded with ball. ... The explosion and the recoil ... so alarmed him, that he turned pale, and put away the gun. As soon as his fear subsided he laughed heartily, as did all his party, and went to examine the wood, which was found to be perforated by the ball. ...
>
> They had some skins of ravens with them, upon which they placed a high price, though being of no use to us, they did not find a purchaser. On several occasions we had noticed the beaks and claws of these birds attached to ornamental bands for the head and waist, and they were evidently considered valuable. (Beechey, 1831:I, 333)

October 2 or 3, 1826: between Sheshalik and Chamisso Island.

The British, returning to the ship in the barge, met a group of natives:
> There were two men whose appearance and conduct again led us to conclude that the large blue glass labrets indicated a superiority of rank, and found, as before, that no reasonable offer would induce them to part with these ornaments. (Beechey, 1831:I, 333)

October 2, 1826: at Chamisso Island

Peard's Journal (1973:170) mentions the visit of an umiak to the ship. It is the last record of such an encounter in 1826.[14]

October 10, 1826: in Eschscholtz Bay.

All the travelling parties of Eskimos had by this date passed the *Blossom* on their return to their winter homes, but the crew of the barge encountered three umiaks with about thirty or forty hostile Buckland River Eskimos who drew their knives and tried to board the vessel (Beechey, 1831:I, 334). Richard Beechey, who witnessed the incident, wrote:
> In their attempts to steal they were unusually daring: one of them on being forced back immediately drew his knife, accompanied with some threats. Mr. Elson declared that he never would have allowed himself to be treated in such a manner with impunity, had he not recollected the obstacles which might be thrown in the way of Capt. Franklin, should a rumor of hostilities between us and the natives get abroad. (Richard Beechey, n.d.:101)

---

[14]Beechey stated that "several" umiaks had visited the ship during his absence—(September 29 to October 3) while he was aboard the barge—and that they sold "a quantity" of dried salmon (1831:I, 333)

The crew of the barge apparently encountered some of the same aggressive Buckland River Eskimos they had met on September 10, and it was probably this same group that had fought with the Russians near the same place in 1820 (see p. 7). Some of these Eskimos later were involved in hostilities with the crew of the *Blossom* on August 14, 1827, and after that were involved in the bloodshed of September 29, 1827, at Chamisso Island (Beechey, 1831:II, 555-59).

A few days later the *Blossom* sailed out of the Arctic because of the fast-approaching winter. Beechey was intent on returning in the following summer.

1827

The BLOSSOM—*August 3-September 10, 1827*

On this return to the Bering Strait region, Beechey continued to search for Franklin's expedition and to chart the coast.

August 3, 1827: at Cape Rodney.

The Barge was hoisted out and ordered to sail north, searching for Port Clarence. Some winter houses were seen (Beechey, 1831:II, 531).

August 11, 1827: at Chamisso Island.

Peard reported seeing one umiak being paddled near shore (1973:228).

The barge arrived from south of Bering Strait, and Elson confirmed the existence of the body of water that Beechey was to name Port Clarence.

August 13, 1827: at Chamisso Island.

Two umiaks visited the ship, and the sailors recognized some of their "old friends" from the year before (Peard, 1973:228). One man offered to trade a muskrat skin for Captain Beechey's epaulettes (Wolfe, n.d.:196). Members of this group had been among the thirty or forty who had threatened to attack the barge in Eschscholtz Bay on October 10, 1826; later, some were involved in the hostilities of September 29, 1827, at Chamisso Island (Beechey, 1831:II, 555-59).

August 14, 1827: at Chamisso Island.

Some of the natives again came to the ship to trade. One of them drew his knife on Peard (Beechey, 1831:II, 555), who wrote that "one or two of them [were] inclined to be troublesome" (Peard, 1973:228). The Captain, not trusting them, thought this group was "dirty, noisy, and impudent." They left the ship late at night but returned a few hours later and found the sailors washing the decks:

> They probably expected that we should be fast asleep, and that they would have an opportunity of appropriating to themselves some of the moveable articles upon deck. There was otherwise no reason for returning so soon; and from what we afterwards saw of these people, there is every reason to believe that was their real motive. (Beechey, 1831:II, 535-36)

August 16, 1827: off Cape Blossom.

Peard (1973:228) reported that ten umiaks were seen and that a few reached the ship to barter fox and beaver skins. Wolfe mentioned that fish were also traded (n.d.:196).[15]

August 25, 1827: at Cape Krusenstern.

Natives were seen on the shore drying "fish and skins" (Peard, 1973:230). In the evening two fires were noticed on shore; and on the supposition that they might be signals from Franklin's party, the ship was hove to. To the disappointment of the British, nothing more unusual was found than that a group of Eskimos had come to the ship for barter (Beechey, 1831:II, 538; Peard, 1973:230).

August 27, 1827: off Choris Peninsula.

A fire and eight or ten people were seen on a cliff of the peninsula, but after sending a boat ashore, the sailors found that it was another native group signalling their desire to trade for tobacco (Beechey, 1831:II, 539; Peard, 1973:230).

August 31-September 6, 1827: in Port Clarence.

The *Blossom* was first anchored in the southeastern corner of the harbour, and some Eskimos visited the ship. Peard noticed "several" boats and tents on shore (1973:231).

Captain Beechey, after several days of survey, estimated that the whole population of the Port Clarence area was about four hundred people who resided in three villages: one on the north spit at Grantley Harbor, one on the north side of Port Clarence, where a "great many" winter houses and burials were seen (Peard, 1973:231), and one at the entrance to the Tuksuk Channel. They found that the natives were well supplied with iron: one girl had a musket hammer hanging from her neck, others had brass-inlaid, iron-headed spears.

> Among the inhabitants of the village on the northern shore, named Choonowuck [Singuk (Ray, 1964:75)], there were several girls with massive iron bracelets. One had a curb chain for a necklace, and another a bell suspended in front, in the manner described in the preceding year at Choris Peninsula. (Beechey, 1831:II, 541-42)[16]

And Peard observed that the natives had, besides their usual weapons,

> long hunting spears armed with iron heads shaped like a sergeant's halberd, and kept remarkably bright and sharp pointed. Indeed we always found them very careful in this particular, frequently trying bits of skin over stone-headed arrows & spears to preserve them from injury. We got from them a few Otter skins &c. Tobacco, buttons, pins & blue beads being as usual in great request. A woman had accidentally seen one of our kettles, and wanted very much to get it, but this we could not part with. (Peard, 1973:231)

The sailors also found that the Eskimos had a good idea of the relative values of their furs: Beechey noted that the price for grey fox or otter skins was a hatchet apiece (1831:II, 542).

A boat from the ship also explored the Tuksuk Channel, and this was reported by Wolfe:

> The shores were mud cliffs and thickly covered with tents of natives who appeared to be collected for the purpose of catching fish; no yourts [winter houses] were seen, therefore it must evidently be a mere

[15]Wolfe, in his journal (n.d.:196) placed the date as August 14 for the purchase of fish, but he was probably incorrect. He also recorded eleven, not ten umiaks.

[16]Beechey also mentioned seeing a dancing house (*kazgi*) at the village.

summer establishment, the salmon were hanging up to dry in great plenty of which the Master purchased a quantity and a Kaiack for which he gave a hatchet—The tents were divided into villages the whole number of inhabitants were estimated at 200 with 25 [umiaks]. The dogs were with them but no sledges were seen, at one of the villages a singular instance of disregard to old age & infirmity was observed in the persons of two females who appeared to be banished from the rest in separate tents just large enough to contain them; they were both without any article of clothing and were labouring under some disease which had rendered the lower part of the face one mass of ulcer, and left the gums exposed. (Wolfe, n.d.:198-99)

Some of the Eskimos they met remembered the sailors from the year before:

Upon the low point at the entrance to the inner harbour, called Nooke by the natives, there were some Esquimaux fishermen, who reminded us of a former acquaintance at Chamisso Island, and saluted us so warmly that we felt sorry their recollection had not entirely failed them. They appeared to have established themselves upon the point for the purpose of catching and drying fish; and from the number of salmon that were leaping in the channel, we should have thought they might have been more successful. They had, however, been fortunate in taking plenty of cod, and some species of salmon trout: they had also caught some herrings.

We were also recognised by a party from the southern shores of the harbour, who, the preceding year, had extended their fishing excursions from this place to Kotzebue Sound. They were some of the most cleanly and well-dressed people we had seen any where on the coast. Their residence was at [Cape Prince of Wales]—a place which, judging from the respectability of parties from that place, whom we had seen elsewhere, must be of importance among the Esquimaux villages upon this coast. (Beechey, 1831:II, 543)

September 10, 1827: at Choris Peninsula.

The ship arrived from Port Clarence, and Captain Beechey learned of the wreck of the barge and of other events during its voyage. The accounts follow.

THE BARGE—*August 3-September 10, 1827*

The barge, under the command of Thomas Elson, was hoisted out from the *Blossom* on August 3, 1827, at Cape Rodney. Beechey ordered Elson to explore the harbour which Beechey was later to name Port Clarence.

August 3, 1827: near Cape Douglas.

The crew visited a vacant house and took some spears, nets and "other trifles", leaving beads in payment (Wolfe, n.d.:195).

August 5, 1827: in Port Clarence.

On the east shore of the harbour the sailors saw two umiaks with ten men in one and ten men and two women in the other. They tried to trade with the latter for an otter skin; and the natives showed that they had clearly established in their own minds the relative values of certain trade items. Wolfe wrote that they wanted

... a fine sea otter skin which the owner seemed well aware was valuable, beads he entirely rejected, a hatchet was then offered, which I think would have gained it, had he not unfortunately espied a small sauce pan; afterwards nothing else would please him; but as the useful utensil could not be spared, he went away with his skin. (Wolfe, n.d.:195)

August 11, 1827: at Chamisso Island.

When the barge joined the *Blossom*, Elson reported to the Captain about Port Clarence. He added that they had met some natives there, one of whom had drawn a map of the area that corresponded to the outline done at Chamisso by the natives from Cape Prince of Wales (p. 17) (Beechey, 1831:II, 534).

August 18, 1827: between Cape Beaufort and Point Lay.

The barge and the *Blossom* had left Kotzebue Sound on August 14 and had sailed northward searching for Franklin. Three days later the command of the barge for its second northerly exploration was given to Belcher on his request. On August 18, three umiaks were met and the sailors purchased three dozen ducks from them (Belcher, n.d.:192).

August 19, 1827: at Icy Cape.

On reaching Icy Cape about twenty natives, including children, were seen. Belcher noted that they had two umiaks and some tents. He found a number of ruined houses that were being used as storage cellars and consequently were filled with meat and blubber (Belcher, n.d.:192). This was probably the village of Kayaakseravik (Spencer, 1959:8; Stefansson, 1909:601-10).

It was possibly in regard to this village that Bechervaise set down some of his observations; these, nevertheless, may have been written as many as ten years after the voyage, and hence should not be accepted uncritically. His account describes the houses in a village eight miles north of Icy Cape. According to Bechervaise, there were fifteen to twenty houses in the settlement, and one, which he measured, was 8 feet square by 6½ feet high:

> From side to side were placed rafters, much the same as the roof of an English house, but with less elevation at the top; across these again were other pieces of scantling both to strengthen the other and secure them; in the middle of the top was a square hole with a frame to it, much like the combings of a hatchway. On top of the rafters were laid the hides of the [walrus], and over that, where it could be got, was turf.... The square part at the top was covered with a double hide and served for the purpose of going in and out or letting the smoke out if required: the stiff hide acted as a spring, for, as the Esquimaux head vanished under, it was closed and perfectly secure.... The inside, on the ground, was thickly strewed with moss; at the sides and ends were seats left in the earth fourteen inches broad, which were also covered with moss over which were laid rein deer skins; the sides were also lined with rein deer skins, which, from the thickness of the hair, are very warm. From the centre of the roof was suspended a stone, like a frying-pan in shape with three holes, to which were fastened three thongs of [walrus] hide, by which it was suspended. In this stone was put a piece of whale's blubber, in the middle of which a hole was cut; in this hole a piece of moss was put and set fire to, which gave a beautiful bright shining light, superior to gas, and without smoke, which from its closeness, warmed the house. At the sides were hung spears, bows and arrows, implements of fishing or household use. On one of the sides of the house was a square hole cut, in which the inhabitants stowed their winter supply of food as well for themselves as for their dogs. In the corner I observed a sort of tunnel which I supposed led to other houses, so that if my judgment be right they may visit each other without going into the open air; other houses may differ, I saw no more of them. ([Bechervaise], 1839:205-206; see also pp. 124-125 following)

The Eskimos at Icy Cape helped the sailors fill their water casks at a well they had dug in the sand (Beechey, 1831:II, 549-50). The barge then departed for the north, but it was able to go less than thirty miles before it was stopped by the ice.

August 23, 1827: at Icy Cape.

Belcher returned with the barge to Icy Cape for observations, and Beechey reported that

Lieutenant Belcher's curiosity was here greatly awakened by one of the natives leading him to a large room used by the Esquimaux for dancing, and by searching for a billet of wood, which his gestures implied had been left by some Europeans, but not finding it, he scrutinized several chips which were in the apartment, and intimated that some person had cut it up. This was very provoking, as Lieutenant Belcher naturally recurred to the possibility of Captain Franklin having been there, and after leaving his billet as a memorial, had returned the same route. (Beechey, 1831:II, 550)

It is possible that what Belcher mistook for a record of Franklin may, in fact, have been evidence left by the Vasiliev and Shismarev expedition.

August 29, 1827: at Point Hope.

When the barge arrived at Point Hope, Belcher found the Eskimos there were preparing their houses for the winter. He bought some "nephrite axes" from them. He also examined some of the dwellings and found that they differed from other Eskimo houses he had seen. In his private journal, some of which is reprinted below, he placed in quotation marks certain passages that he had drawn from his report to Beechey:

"... I examined four or five of these inhabited and was much surprised to find so much neatness, cleanliness and comfort in the great apartment, although the entrance was much the reverse. In the principal one I examined, I had to descend from the summit of the flat of the Mound through a sort of well formed of stone, about 8 feet deep, but furnished at the bottom with two large whale vertebra for the purpose of a step. The passage then runs (about 3 feet high & the same in width) a little on the descent for 6 feet, then the same at the opposite angle ascent, at the end of which at the top, was a hole about 2 feet diameter through the flooring, which opened into an apartment about 10 feet square and the same in height, the back half being fitted as a kind of standing bed-place, the floor remarkably clean, and of smooth fir plank, the light afforded by a square hole at the apex covered with the gut similar to the skin dresses, and in one corner stood a receptacle similar to the font in Roman Catholic Churches in which was seal oil with a ridge of wick alight on its outer edge. The temperature was very oppressive to the lungs and when I examined [the interior of the house] a second time through the window at the summit [the air] was insupportable" (Belcher, n.d.:201-202)

As they differ from those I have before examined I have inserted the plan & section (Plate XIII). It is really astonishing how they manage to keep *the* apartment clean, whilst the entrance is so very dirty, as from the height, they must of necessity crawl on their knees, and the flooring of several were pretty well be smeared with oil &c.

"They were all anxious to show me the [houses] and followed from one to another. At length I came to one of large dimensions, half filled with sledges &c, which by their gestures appeared (like that of Icy

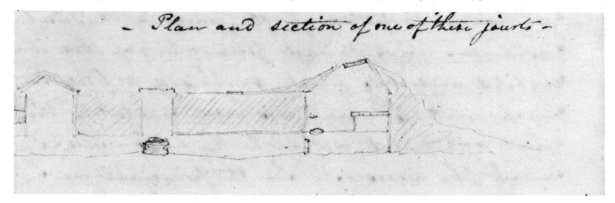

Plate XIII Belcher's plan of a house at Point Hope, August 29th, 1827. By courtesy of the University of British Columbia Library.

Cape) to be their dancing room, being about 30 feet square entrance very large, and unfurnished beyond the flooring."

It is impossible to mistake their gestures and signs for its being a dancing room as the song, and turn of the body and arms, are too expressive. Several frames of tambourins were hung up within. (Belcher, n.d.:202)

Belcher's descriptions are particularly interesting because the type of structure he described and the house Smyth described on August 19, 1826, north of Icy Cape (pp.176-77) differ in important ways from the house Bechervaise described at Icy Cape on August 19, 1827 (p. 123). Bechervaise, for instance, did not mention an entry hole in the floor of the main room of the house, floor boards, or a sleeping platform, and Smyth and Belcher failed to note moss floors or caribou skin linings on the walls.

The dwellings described by Smyth and Belcher correspond closely to the houses described by a number of people for coast-dwelling Eskimos, whereas the structure described by Bechervaise bears reasonable similarity to the *paamerak*, a type of dwelling used by Eskimos whose economy was oriented more to the interior than to the coast. According to Spencer, a *paamerak* was

a more permanent sod house, suggestive of the coastal dwellings . . . a house built to last longer than one winter and usually erected at a more permanent site, such as at a fishing station or in the neighborhood of a caribou stockade. The plan made use of a passageway leading into the house although the more elaborate wooden interiors of the coastal people were lacking. Similarly, while an excavation might be made for this type of dwelling, it rarely went to a depth of more than a few inches. . . . A double paamerak, with a short passage leading from that which connected the two apartments, was also known.

The permanent sod structures were thus built with a passage and a skylight and had banked areas of sod placed along the side walls for sleeping and reclining. A fireplace was located under the skylight, the gut window being rolled back when fires were built and serving as a smokehole. General heating was done with the stone lamp. (Spencer, 1959:47)

Paameraks were never high; about five feet on the inside was the average dimension (Spencer, 1959:48). They were covered on the inside with caribou skins for insulation (Spencer, 1959:45).

September 3, 1827: on Choris Peninsula.

Near Point Garnet Belcher met an Eskimo family consisting of an old man, his wife, and two girls. They told him that two Eskimos had drowned in a gale when their umiak upset (Belcher, n.d.:207).

September 7, 1827: on Choris Peninsula.

While Belcher was hauling wood to build an observatory on Choris Peninsula, a strong southwest wind sprang up suddenly and resulted in a heavy sea's battering the barge, which was anchored in shallow water; because of the steep swells it soon struck bottom and filled with water. Belcher tried to save the crew on board by reaching the barge with the boat, but the boat became badly damaged by the waves on launching. Some Eskimos with an umiak were nearby, and were apparently aware of the futility of trying to launch a boat in the gale. Belcher, however, forced them at pistol point to carry the boat to the water, and then he launched it twice, unsuccessfully, with a crew of sailors and Eskimos (Belcher, n.d.:211; Wolfe, n.d.:200).

The barge was a total loss and three of the crew were drowned. The natives gave the shipwrecked sailors some fish, but when Belcher tried to buy some fur trousers, he found that the price had risen from two strings of beads before the accident to three strings afterwards (Belcher, n.d.:216; Wolfe, n.d.:200-201).

September 9, 1827: on Choris Peninsula.

The large amounts of brass and iron in the barge caused the Eskimos to salvage pieces from the wreckage. Belcher considered this vandalism and forced them to return as much as he could. He was of the opinion that this group of Eskimos understood the capabilities of his pistols, for one of the group offered a knife and other items in trade for a pistol (Belcher, n.d.:221; Wolfe n.a.:200).

September 10, 1827: on Choris Peninsula.

On the day of the *Blossom*'s arrival at the Chamisso anchorage, the group of Eskimos visiting the wreck had increased to twenty-four with the landing of two umiaks. Thus the sailors were outnumbered three to one. The scavenging increased and two of the Eskimos, from whom the sailors tried to take the wreckage, drew their knives on them. Belcher kept the natives under control with his pistols; he was, fortunately, on good terms with the Eskimo leader who persuaded one of the men to withdraw, but the other remained with his knife drawn. When a boat arrived from the ship, Belcher ordered him taken aboard and kept in captivity until some of the goods were returned. This man was so strong that it required six of the boat's crew to carry him off. When this abduction occurred, all the Eskimos except the man's family and the leader left the area (Peard, 1973:234; Wolfe, n.d.:201; see also pages 216-16).[17] Wolfe's account follows:

> The natives picked up what things drifted on shore particularly pleased with the iron and copper and even went off to get what they could from the wreck. This very natural conduct appears to have excited the displeasure of Lieut. Belcher, and when our cutter landed he made signal for more assistance & fire arms, he supposing that if one of the natives were seized and taken on board every thing would be returned. (Wolfe, n.d.:200-01)

THE BLOSSOM—*September 11-October 5, 1827*

September 11, 1827: at Chamisso Island.

Belcher described these events the day after the Eskimo was taken captive:
> During the day . . . I visited the wreck to ascertain if I could recover any of my most valuable articles supposed to be still in her, and as the party might still be encamped on the beach took with me the Prisoner.
>
> Previous to this two [umiaks] had visited the Ship during which time the prisoner had not been allowed to communicate with them. They had nearly reached the shore when the prisoner signified to me that his wife was in one of them. I immediately pointed out where they had gone and as it lay in our route permitted him to hail them en passant which at this time they did not seem to notice. On passing the spot where I had expected to find the Old Chief I was surprised to find he had decamped leaving the property of the others (who fled) behind, as well as several of their dogs.
>
> By the time we arrived at the wreck I observed the two [umiaks] beforementioned coming around Pt. Garnet and after passing the property beforementioned without disturbing it, came down to us, where his wife soon recognised, and was almost frantic on perceiving him a prisoner. The [umiak] in which she was remained, but the other pulled off toward the west, from whence I observed another coming.

[17]Peard recorded that the man's family remained on the beach, but Beechey (1831:II, 552-54) did not mention this.

Wishing to give him all the advantage I could of communicating with his friends, I got the [umiak] alongside where they remained quietly for some time until they fancied we were off our guard. Suddenly the prisoner leaped into the [umiak]. I happened to perceive his intention and leaping at the same instant into her stern, presented one pistol at him, had my knee on the steersman chest, and the other pistol at his mouth, which so completely astonished them that no effort was made to push off, and the bowman with his boathook immediately pulling her alongside the prisoner was placed in statu quo—. The [umiak] which had pulled off as well as the other observed, now joined, and although we had force sufficient to conquer treble the numbers, still I deemed it prudent (as my orders relative to the Prisoner were strict) to cut off all hope of his release. I therefore landed and made the boat keep off, making the other parties understand, I would communicate with *them* on shore. The [umiak] I had observed to come from the westward contained nearly the whole of the depredatory gang. The old man the *father* of the prisoner was among them, and almost smothered me with caresses, at the same time signifying he had brought back part of the stolen property. They brought me three bags which I motioned them to turn out on one of their large deer skins on the beach, the contents rather disappointed me being only part of the iron work cut from the Barge's greer &c. The Old man then offered me skins of various kinds and used every effort to induce me to release my prisoner but finding me inexorable, signified a wish to supply him with fresh fur dresses and deer skins for bed [.] This I acceded to, but with precaution. I then made the old man understand that I should return on the morrow, and if he brought the other private property which had been stolen, would release the Prisoner. On my departure they set up a most woeful cry in which the women and dogs joined chorus, adding much to the distress of the Prisoner who appeared very much affected and cried bitterly.

They soon began to follow us and making fresh signs they wished to give him more clothes I again permitted the [umiak] in which his father was to come alongside, when the old man's caresses were repeated in the most earnest manner, and had I possessed the power, certainly should have released the Prisoner, as at this moment, the effect would have softened the rupture and given them a much stronger idea of our clemency. Finding they had only made this a pretext to gain ground I again caused their departure, as I began to feel uncomfortable under present circumstances and much regretted my inability to restore him, my orders being most *positive* "not to permit his escape & bring him back".

I now perceived him making preparations to leap overboard (having stripped) and ordering our crew to pull hard fired a pistol over the heads of those astern, at the same time pointing another at the prisoner, who now dressed himself and gave up all hopes. The [umiak] parties now set up a fresh lamentation joined by the dogs on shore as well as those afloat which with the tears of the Prisoner made one stretch out to distance them which to my relief we very soon did, when the Prisoner quietly pulled an oar and regained his good humour.

To my signs to come to the ship and we would restore the prisoner, they did not either understand or perhaps think proper to place any reliance on, being perfectly unacquainted with the probable fate of our Prisoner whom I have not the least doubt they now gave up as lost for ever. The prisoner however must have communicated with them, and from the treatment he experienced on board could not have omitted to acquaint his friends how little they had to fear for his life. (Belcher, n.d.:229-32)

September 12, 1827: at Chamisso Island.

The group that had been waiting on shore for the captive Eskimo departed (Peard, 1973:235).

September 13, 1827: at Chamisso Island.

On the thirteenth the Eskimo who had been detained was released and sent ashore. Wolfe wrote a fitting summation of the incident:
... we found no benefit arising from the method we had pursued. The fact was Lieut. Belcher was a great loser by this unfortunate accident and among other things was a valuable theodolite which he suspected to be in the hands of these natives, but I believe it was not the case. Whilst the hostage was

detained on board, he was treated with the greatest kindness, and many presents made him, yet he evinced a very natural dislike to his situation, and would frequently burst into tears; probably the idea of captivity was before unknown to him, and the uncertainty of his fate with the absence from his family & friends must have awakened a new train of feelings, powerful enough to unman a mind supported by the aid of religion or philosophy. When he was liberated many contributed to make up a quantity of beads, tobacco &c &c and I confess I was heartily glad to see him free. When landed it appears his own party were not on the spot, but he joined another, and would doubtless soon find his friends. (Wolfe, n.d.:200:01)

Later, two umiaks came alongside the ship. Beechey remembered some of the Eskimos from the group that had threatened the barge in Eschscholtz Bay on October 10, 1826, and had later acted in a hostile manner aboard the *Blossom* on August 14, 1827 (Beechey, 1831:II, 555). As told by Peard, the visit was amicable, but in the evening, when the sailors wanted the natives to leave, the peace was ended:

They took no notice of our signs but when the Gunner motioned to them with a cutlass, they got ready their bows and shewed they were determined to have their own way. However, on a musket or two being levelled at them they made off, but held up their weapons in defiance, pointing to the shore, and uttering what we constructed from their gestures to be threats and imprecations. (Peard, 1973:235)

Beechey noted that when a musket was pointed at them, they shot an arrow into the water in the direction of the ship and then went to the island, where they made camp (1831:II, 555).

September 14, 1827: at Chamisso Island.

On the following day hostilities increased between the two groups. By their actions the Eskimos showed that they clearly understood the use of firearms. A watering party consisting of two midshipmen and sixteen men had been sent ashore near the Eskimo camp, and Smyth, who had charge of the party,

was desired to arm his people, and to order the Esquimaux off the island if they were offensive to him, or interfered with the duty. On landing, the natives met him on the beach, and were very anxious to learn whether the muskets were loaded, and to be allowed to feel the edges of the cutlasses, and were not at all pleased at having their request refused. (Beechey, 1831:II, 555)

Smyth wrote:

The natives came to us, and one being determined to examine the contents of the foresail which I had caused to be carried on shore to cover the arms, the man who had charge thereof resisted and the native immediately drew his knife; seeing this I ordered the crews to take their arms & load, the natives then fled to their tents, launched their boats & put everything into them. Thinking they were going I stopt the pursuit, but observing them return with their bows, making warlike signs, I ordered our people to advance and when within 10 or 12 yards the natives stopped drawn up in a line, and an old man came forward making signs that he wanted a tub which he had left at the brook; this I ordered to be brought and returned to him. His companions were during this interval in readiness with their arrows in the bows pointed towards us and their naked knives grasped in the right hand. On receiving the tub, the old man made signs of friendship and his party returned their bows & arrows, after remaining a short time in this situation I left them to complete our watering, they soon followed bringing their bows, which however after a little consultation among themselves were laid aside. They endeavoured to persuade us to ground our arms, but I would not permit it. (Smyth, n.d.*b*:201-02)

Beechey added:

A few minutes before this occurred, five of the party, who had separated from their companions, attacked two of our seamen, who were at some distance from Mr. Smyth, digging a grave for their unfortunate shipmate, and coming suddenly upon them, while in the pit, three of the party stood over the workmen with their drawn knives, while the others rifled the pockets of their jackets, which were lying at a little distance from the grave, and carried away the contents, together with an axe. (Beechey, 1831:II, 555-56)

Peard, too, wrote of the event:

> On the return of the watering party, the Captain sent Lieutenant Wainwright and a party of Marines on shore with orders to drive the Natives off the Island, and on resistance to shoot them. In the meantime, however they had taken their departure. (Peard, 1973:236)

Smyth's description of the events is interesting in that it sheds light on Beechey's handling of the matter:

> On hearing the story of their being robbed . . . I then asked which of the natives was the most forward in the robbery but they could not point out any particular one and Mr. Rendell agreeing with me that as we were not able to make them sensible of the outrage they had committed it would be a pity to commence an attack in which no doubt all of them would have fallen a sacrifice to their audacity and with a great probability of losing several of our own crew. After we had left the beach the [umiak] pulled over to Escholtz Bay & I felt very happy in concluding an affair so amicably which had at the outset such an appearance of bloodshed; I consider myself much indebted to Mr. Rendell for his advice during the transaction. My conduct was however considered blamiable by the Captain, who thought that I had done wrong in not having punished them for the misdemeanor, but I appeal to the feelings of any man whether they would under all circumstances have renewed a quarrel, the sanguinary results of which were so apparent. (Smyth, n.d.b:202)

Wolfe added some important information.

> It was proved afterwards that the seamen had very much magnified both the loss they had sustained and the nature of the robbery, indeed so contradictory were the evidences that it remained doubtful whether any thing of the kind had taken place or not. Altho the fact of so daring an outrage upon any one of us deserved severe notice, yet I cannot but agree with Mr. Smyth in his ideas, considering all the circumstances under which he was placed. (Wolfe, n.d.:202)

Certainly many of the Eskimos encountered by the *Blossom*'s crew were unaware of the use of guns, but the behaviour of the Buckland River natives strongly suggests that they were acquainted with the capabilities of firearms. Captain Gray had traded guns and ammunition to this group in 1819 and it is possible that other traders were operating in the Bering Strait region about the same time (Ray, 1975).

The knowledge of firearms was not restricted to the Buckland River Eskimos. When Beechey and Osmer compiled a short vocabulary for a group of Eskimos from Cape Prince of Wales, they found that the natives used the word "Kee-suk" to designate gun (Beechey, 1831:II, 622). These Eskimos may have obtained their knowledge of firearms on the west side of Bering Strait, because Kotzebue saw a native with a musket at Cape Dezhnev in 1816 (Kotzebue, 1821:I, 245). In 1828 Lütke found that the coastal natives of the Chuktosk Peninsula definitely associated Europeans with firearms:

> Ils n'ont pas jusqu'ici de fusils, et ils les craignent même, parce qu'il est défendu de leur vendae dans les foires des armees à feu; et ce n'est pas, par consequent, sans raison qu'ils nous appellent jusqu'à présent les *hommes de feu.* (Lütke, 1835:II, 266-27)

With the advent of the whaling fleet to Bering Strait after 1848, contacts between the natives and whalers and traders became frequent. The first of a regular supply of firearms probably reached Point Hope and Cape Prince of Wales in the 1860s (Driggs, 1905:95; Thornton, 1931:139).

September 18, 1827: near Elephant Point.

A crew in the barge was sent to examine the "ice cliffs" in Eschscholtz Bay. About three or four miles beyond Elephant Point Peard noticed "several deserted huts built of wood & filled in with turf" (1973:236).

September 29, 1827: at Chamisso Island.

On the 29th of September the animosity between the British sailors and the Buckland River Eskimos—which had been smouldering for a fortnight—broke out and resulted in the death of one of the natives: this was the first recorded killing in northern Alaska between Eskimos and Europeans.

A watering party was on shore at Chamisso when the sailors on board the ship noticed an umiak with eight men and a boy heading to the island. In response, Peard sent the cutter with an armed crew under Belcher's command to protect the sailors on shore (Wolfe, n.d.:203); ordering Belcher to drive the Eskimos away if they "proved to be any of the same party that had so lately distinguished themselves for daring and insolence" (Peard, 1973:239).

The Eskimos reached the island before the cutter and had already begun to barter with the sailors. According to Wolfe:

> Mr. Osmer who met them, thought they were very friendly disposed, wishing to exchange some skins and even their bows for tobacco, but he was not provided, and when he parted from them he thought they were going off to the Ship. Mr. Osmer only recognized one among this party who had accompanied the last audacious set, but on that occasion he appeared to be a principal hand, he was pointed out to Mr. Belcher, who obliged him to put down a piece of wood with some iron nails, which he was carrying off, this he seemed to take very much amiss. (Wolfe, n.d.:203)

It was later learned that the piece of wood had been given to the Eskimo by one of the midshipmen, who was in charge of the watering party (Peard, 1973:239).

The Eskimos then went back to their umiaks and the sailors pushed it off, but the natives paddled back to shore and were pushed out again. This was repeated a number of times (Wolfe, n.d.:203). According to the Captain, while this was going on the Eskimos "were occupied in preparations for hostility, by putting on their eider-duck frocks over their usual dresses, and uncovering their bows and arrows" (Beechey, 1831:II, 556). They then

> paddled a few yards from the beach, and then rested in doubt as to what they should do; some menacing our party, and others displaying their weapons. Thus threatened, and the party making no attempt to depart, but rather propelling their [umiak] sidewise toward the land, Mr. Belcher fired a ball between them and the shore, and waved them to begone. (Beechey, 1831:II, 556-57)
>
> ... they instantly ran the [umiak] on shore, wrapped an extra skin round them, jumped out with their weapons and gaining a neighbouring cliff, discharged their arrows at a distance of 130 paces wounded one of our people in the thigh. (Peard, 1973:239)[18]
>
> ... orders were then given to fire and an unfortunate native who had remained behind for the purpose (as it was afterwards found) of cutting a hole in the [umiak], was struck in the leg, yet he limped off and joined his companions, who then made a retreating flight into one of the gullies firing arrows occasionally. By this time we had a gun ready from the Ship and perceiving the natives crawling over the brow of a cliff fired a shot at them, which tho' it fell short, evidently threw them into the greatest consternation, and they ran to & fro not knowing where to go. When the firing had ceased Mr. Belcher divided his party consisting now of 21 persons (five of the officers who had been sporting having joined) into two intending to proceed to the assistance of the Master & Purser who were on the other side of the island in the direction which some of the natives seemed to have taken, when the second Cutter arrived with these officers in her accompanying the Captain to whom the boat had been sent on perceiving that hostilities had commenced for at this time he was in one of the small bays making observations. When all the circumstances had been reported to him, he took the command and ascended the hill, purposing to secure the persons of the natives and take them on board the Ship. A small party consisting of the Serjeant & four marines was detached along the edge of the Cliff to reconnoitre, while the main body was about 30 yards within them; in this manner they had not advanced more than 20 yards, when a cry was heard, and three of the five marines were seen stretched on the ground, one of them had received an arrow thro' the arm which transfixed it to his side, another in the head and a third

---

[18]Beechey records that two people were wounded by arrows in the initial flight (1831:II, 557).

a little above the wrist; a fourth was also struck on the wrist but owing to his being very thickly clothed just on the spot the arrow scarcely raised the skin. (Wolfe, n.d.:203)

The natives had been lying concealed by tall grass in a small ravine. They fired on the marines from only five or six yards away (Beechey, 1831:II, 557; Peard, 1973:239). Then

The marines fired their pieces, shot away two of their bayonets and were ordered to fall back. Mr. Elson hastening to the spot where he observed the firing, and approaching close to the same ravine but on the other side of it saw three fellows adjusting their arrows; he immediately leveled his piece at one of them not more than half a dozen yards off, gave the poor wretch the contents (a ball over a charge of duck shot) and retreated to the rest of the party. (Peard, 1973:239-40)

After the firing, which was intended "more to alarm than to destroy", Beechey ordered his men to lay down their arms (Wolfe, n.d.:203). The Captain then advanced alone toward the Eskimos

and made signs of friendship, this however had no other effect than that they forbore firing, and it was not until an hour had elapsed that one of them ventured cautiously to raise his head. . . . During the above time we perceived them busy in making a sort of breast work across the only part of the gully we could command, with mud and clods of earth. (Wolfe, n.d.:203-04)

Beechey's narrative stated that:

After a considerable time, an elderly man came forward with his arms and breast covered with mud, motioning to us to begone, and decidedly rejecting all offers of reconciliation. Unwilling to chastise them further, I withdrew the party, and towed their [umiak] on board, which kept them prisoners upon the island. I did this in order to have an opportunity of bringing about a reconciliation, for I was unwilling to allow them to depart with sentiments which might prove injurious to any Europeans who might succeed us; and I thought that by detaining them we should be able to convince them our resentment was unjustifiably provoked, and that when they conducted themselves properly, they should command our friendship. (Beechey, 1831:II, 557)

The umiak was then repaired on board and made ready for its return to the Eskimos (Beechey, 1831:II, 558).

September 30, 1827: at Chamisso Island.

A boat was sent to the island to prevent the Eskimos from escaping or being relieved. Two Eskimos were seen briefly. In the evening, when the temperature fell below 30°F., Beechey sent their skins and some seal meat to the island. These were left in front of a fire, and the boat departed for the night (Peard, 1973:240; Wolfe, n.d.:204).

October 1, 1827: at Chamisso Island.

In the morning, when the boat returned to the island, it was found that the Eskimos had not taken the meat or skins. Their umiak, which had been repaired, was left for them with some tobacco and beads to pay for three knives and some bows and arrows that Beechey confiscated (Peard, 1973:240; Wolfe, n.d.:204).

October 2, 1827: at Chamisso Island.

The sailors noticed that the umiak had been moved and was hidden in some bushes at another part of the island. In the evening it was gone.

October 5, 1827: at Chamisso Island.

On the last day that the *Blossom* was in the Arctic, Peard went ashore at Chamisso:

At 5 PM. Mr. Elson, Mr. Collie and myself obtained leave to examine the ravine the scene of action on Chamisso Island. We found that part of it where the marines were wounded, three or four feet deep, and two holes on one side and three on the other dug partly under the bank, free from snow, large enough to hold one or two persons in a sitting posture, and in a single instance communicating with each other under ground.

Here we discovered a poor fellow laying under the snow athwart the ditch most likely in the same position he fell after receiving the fatal wounds, three of which we remarked on his face, as if from buck shot. His quiver full of arrows remained slung at his back and his bow had been placed under his head. My companions recognized him as one of the leaders in the late fray; and no doubt he met his death from Mr. Elson's gun. Several broken arrows were laying about the Spot. (Peard, 1973:241)

Later in the evening the *Blossom* sailed from Kotzebue Sound; no other British ships were to pass north of Bering Strait for more than two decades.

BIBLIOGRAPHY

Armstrong, Alexander
1857   *A Personal Narrative of Discovery of the Northwest Passage;* London, Hurst and Blackett
Armstrong, Terence
1965   *Russian Settlement in the North;* Cambridge, Cambridge University Press
Arutiounov, S.A., and Sergeev, D.A.
1969   *Drevnie Kulturi Aziatshik Eskimosov;* Moscow, Akademia Nauk
Ashley, Clifford
1944   *Clifford Ashley's Book of Knots;* Garden City, Doubleday
Ashmolean Museum
1836   *A Catalogue of the Ashmolean Museum;* Oxford, Collingwood
Bailey, A.M., and Hendee, R.W.
1926   "Notes on the Mammals of Northwestern Alaska"; *Journal of Mammology*, vol. 7, no.1
Baker, Marcus
1906   *Geographic Dictionary of Alaska;* 2nd. ed.; Washington, D.C., U.S. Government Printing Office
Bandi, Hans-Georg
1956   "Einige Gegenstände aus Alaska und Britisch Kolumbien, Gesammelt von Johann Wäber . . . 1776-1780"; *Proceedings of the Thirty-Second International Congress of Americanists;* Copenhagen, Munksgaard
Beaglehole, J.C.
1966   *The Exploration of the Pacific;* 3rd ed.; Stanford, Stanford University Press
1967   *The Journals of Captain James Cook: The Voyage of the "Resolution" and "Discovery", 1776-1780;* Cambridge, Hakluyt Society
[Bechervaise, John]
1839   *Thirty-Six Years of a Seafaring Life;* London, Woodward
Beechey, Frederick William
1831   *Narrative of a Voyage to the Pacific and Beering's Strait* . . . ; London, Colburn and Bentley
n.d.   Sketches; Archives of the Hydrographer of the Navy, Taunton, Somerset
Beechey, Richard
n.d.   "Remarks on a Voyage of Discovery to the Pacific and Bhering's Straits on board H.M.S. Blossom by Rich. Beechey Midn., aged 15"; Public Record Office of Northern Ireland, Belfast
Belcher, Edward
1843   *Narrative of a Voyage Round the World, Performed in Her Majesty's Ship Sulphur During the Years 1836-42* . . . ; London, Colburn
1861   "On the Manufacture of Works of Art by the Esquimaux"; *Transactions of the Ethnological Society of London;* n.s. vol. 1
n.d.   "Private Journal, Remarks, etc., HM Ship Blossom on Discovery During the Years 1825, 6, 7 . . . and Continuation of Private Journal . . ."; typescript copy, Special Collections Division, The Library of the University of British Columbia, Vancouver
Birket-Smith, Kaj
1941   "Early Collections from the Pacific Eskimo"; *Ethnographical Studies*, Nationalmuseets Skrifter, Etnografisk Raekke; Copenhagen
1953   *The Chugach Eskimo;* Nationalmuseets Skrifter, Etnografisk Raekke, vol. 6; Copenhagen
Blackwood, Beatrice
1970   "The Origin and Development of the Pitt Rivers Museum"; *Occasional Papers in Technology*, no. 11; Pitt Rivers Museum, University of Oxford
Boas, Franz
1888   "The Central Eskimo"; *Sixth Annual Report of the Bureau of Ethnology, 1884-85;* Washington, D.C., U.S. Government Printing Office
1899   "Property Marks of Alaskan Eskimo"; *American Anthropologist*, n.s. vol. 1

134

1901 "The Eskimo of Baffin Land and Hudson Bay"; *Bulletin of the American Museum of Natural History*, vol. 15, Part I

1908 "Decorative designs of Alaskan needlecases . . ."; *Proceedings of the U.S. National Museum*, vol. 34, Washington, D.C., U.S. Government Printing Office

Bockstoce, John

1973 "Aspects of the Archaeology of Cape Nome, Alaska . . ."; D. Phil. dissertation, Department of Ethnology and Prehistory, University of Oxford

Bogojavlensky, Sergei

1969 "Imaangmiut Skin Boat Careers" Ph.D. dissertation, Department of Anthropology, Harvard University, Cambridge, Massachusetts

Bogoras, W.

1904 *The Chukchee;* Part I, Material Culture (1904); Memoirs of the American Museum of Natural History, vol. 11; New York

Bompas, W.

n.d. "The Esquimaux of the Mackenzie River"; ms., Church Missionary Society, London

Brower, Charles

1899 "Sinew Working at Pt. Barrow"; *American Anthropologist*, n.s. vol. 1

n.d. "The Northernmost American: an Autobiography"; typescript copy, Naval Arctic Research Laboratory, Barrow, Alaska

Buckland, William

1831 "On the Occurrence of the Remains of Elephants, and Other Quadrupeds . . . in Eschscholtz Bay . . ."; in Frederick William Beechey, *Voyage to the Pacific and Beering's Strait* . . . ; 1831, London, Colburn and Bentley

Burch, Ernest

n.d. Personal communication

Bushnell, G.H.S.

1949 "Some Old Western Eskimo Spear-Throwers"; *Man*, vol. 49

Choris, Louis

1822 *Voyage Pittoresque Autour du Monde* . . . ; Paris, Firmin Didot

Cochrane, John

1824 *A Narrative of a Pedestrian Journey Through Russia and Siberian Tartary* . . . ; London, John Murray

Collins, H.B.

1937 *The Archaeology of St. Lawrence Island, Alaska;* Smithsonian Miscellaneous Collections, No. 96, Washington, D.C.

Collins, H.B., and others

1973 *The Far North: 2000 Years of American Eskimo and Indian Art;* National Gallery of Art, Washington, D.C.

Coxe, William

1780 *Account of the Russian Discoveries between Asia and America* . . . ; London, Cadell

Crowe, Keith J.

1969 *A Cultural Geography of Northern Foxe Basin, N.W.T.;* Northern Science Research Group (NSRG 69-2), Department of Indian Affairs and Northern Development; Ottawa

Driggs, John

1905 *Short Sketches from Oldest America;* Philadelphia, George W. Jacobs

Edmonds, H.M.W.

1966 "M.H.W. Edmonds' Report on the Eskimos of St. Michael and Vicinity"; Dorothy Jean Ray (ed.); *Anthropological Papers of the University of Alaska*, vol. 13, no. 2

Elson, Thomas

1973 Log of the voyage of the barge of H.M.S. Blossom, 1826; quoted in: George Peard, *To the Pacific and Arctic with Beechey: The Journal of Lieutenant George Peard of H.M.S. "Blossom" 1825-1828;* Barry Gough, (ed.); Cambridge, Hakluyt Society

Faber, Kurt
1916   *Unter Eskimos und Walfischfangern;* Stuttgart, Robert Lutz
Fagg, William
1972   *Eskimo Art in the British Museum;* London, The Trustees of the British Museum
Fedorova, Svetlana G.
1973   *The Russian Population in Alaska and California: Late 18th Century-1867*; Kingston, Ontario, The Limetone Press
Foote, Don Charles
1965   "Exploration and Resource Utilization in Northwestern Arctic Alaska Before 1855"; Ph.D. dissertation, Department of Geography, McGill University, Montreal
Ford, James
1959   "Eskimo Prehistory in the Vicinity of Point Barrow, Alaska"; *Anthropological Papers of the American Museum of Natural History*, vol. 47, part 1
Franklin, John
1828   *Narrative of a Second Expedition to the Shores of the Polar Sea . . .* ; London, John Murray
Geist, Otto, and Rainey, Froelich
1936   *Archaeological Excavations at Kukulik, St. Lawrence Island, Alaska;* Miscellaneous Publications of the University of Alaska, vol. 2, Washington, D.C., U.S. Government Printing Office
Giddings, J.L.
1952   *The Arctic Woodland Culture of the Kobuk River;* University Museum Monograph Series, University of Pennsylvania
Golder, F.A.
1914   *Russian Expansion on the Pacific 1641-1850;* Cleveland, Arthur H. Clark
Gough, Barry (ed.)
1973   *To the Pacific and Arctic with Beechey: The Journal of Lieutenant George Peard of H.M.S. "Blossom" 1825-1828;* Cambridge, Hakluyt Society
Hakluyt, Richard
1589   *The Principall Navigations, Voiages and Discoveries of the English Nation . . .* ; London
Hall, Edwin S., Jr.
1969   "Avian Remains from the Kangiguksuk Site, Northern Alaska"; *The Condor*, January
n.d.   Personal communication
Hamilton, T.M.
1970   "The Eskimo Bow and the Asiatic Composite"; *Arctic Anthropology*, vol. 6, no. 2
Hoffman, Walter
1897   "The Graphic Art of the Eskimos"; *Annual Report of the U.S. National Museum*, 1895; Washington, D.C., U.S. Government Printing Office
Hooker, W.J.
1841   "*The Botany of Captain Beechey's Voyage . . .* "; London, H.G. Bohn
Hooper, C.L.
1884   *Report of the Cruise of the U.S. Revenue Steamer Thomas Corwin, in the Arctic Ocean, 1881;* Washington, D.C., U.S. Government Printing Office
Hooper, W.H.
1853   *Ten Months among the Tents of the Tuski . . .* ; London, John Murray
Hough, Walter
1898   "The Lamp of the Eskimo"; *The Board of Regents of the Smithsonian Institution . . . 1896 . . . Report of the U.S. National Museum;* Washington, D.C., U.S. Government Printing Office
Howay, F.W.
1973   *A List of Trading Vessels in the Maritime Fur Trade, 1785-1825;* Richard A. Pierce (ed.), Materials for the Study of Alaskan History, No. 2; Kingston, Ontario, The Limestone Press
International Boundary Commission
[1918]   *Joint Report Upon the Survey and Demarcation of the International Boundary Between the United States and Canada along the 141st Meridian . . .* Washington, D.C., U.S. Government Printing Office

Irving, William
1953   *An Archaeological Reconnaissance of the Lower Colville River and Delta Regions;* Final Report for Submission to the Chief of Naval Research; NR 307-206; NONR 773 (oo); Contract Between the Office of Naval Research and the University of Alaska; April

Jefferys, Thomas (trans.)
1761   *Voyages from Asia to America;* by Gerhard Müller, London, Thomas Jeffrys

Jenness, Diamond
1946   "Material Culture of the Copper Eskimo"; *Report of the Canadian Arctic Expedition 1913-1918,* vol. 16; Ottawa, King's Printer

Kirwan, L.P.
1960   *A History of Polar Exploration;* New York, W. W. Norton

Kotzebue, Otto von
1821   *A Voyage of Discovery, into the South Sea and Beering's Straits . . . ;* London, Longman, Hurst, Rees, Orme and Brown

Krause, Aurel, and Krause, Arthur
1882   "Die Wissenschaftliche Expedition . . . Beringsstrasse"; *Deutsche Geographische Blatter*, vol. 5, bind 1; Bremen

Lada-Mocarski, Valerian
1969   *Bibliography of Books on Alaska Published before 1868;* New Haven, Yale University Press

Larsen, Helge
1951   "De dansk-amerikanske Alaska-ekspeditioner 1949-50"; *Geografisk Tidsskrift*, vol. 51
1968   "Near Ipiutak and Uwelen-Okvik"; *Folk;* vol. 10

Larsen, Helge, and Rainey, Froelich
1948   "Ipiutak and the Arctic Whale Hunting Culture"; *Anthropological Papers of the American Museum of Natural History*, vol. 42

Laughton, J.K.
1885   *Dictionary of National Biography;* Leslie Stephen (ed.); vol. 4; London

Lebedev, Dimitri, and Grekov, Vadim
1967   "Geographical Exploration by the Russians"; in Herman Friis (ed.), *The Pacific Basin: A History of Its Geographical Exploration;* New York, American Geographical Society

Ledyard, John
1963   *John Ledyard's Journal of Captain Cook's Last Voyage;* John Kenneth Munford (ed.), Corvallis, Oregon State University Press

Lütke, Frederic
1835   *Voyage Autour du Monde . . . ;* Paris

Macmillan, Donald
1927   *Four Years in the White North;* Boston, Houghton Mifflin

Mason, O.T.
1885   "Throwing-Sticks in the National Museum"; *Annual Report of the U.S. National Museum, 1884;* Washington, D.C., U.S. Government Printing Office
1901   "Aboriginal Skin-Dressing . . ."; *Annual Report of the U.S. National Museum, 1899;* Washington, D.C., U.S. Government Printing Office
1902   "Aboriginal American Harpoons . . ."; *Annual Report of the U.S. National Museum, 1900;* Washington, D.C., U.S. Government Printing Office

Masterson, James, and Brower, Helen
1948   *Bering's Successors 1745-1780 . . . ;* Seattle, University of Washington Press

Murdoch, John
1884   "Fish and Fishing at Point Barrow, Arctic Alaska"; *Transactions of the American Fish Cultural Association;* Thirteenth Annual Meeting, New York
1885   "A Study of Eskimo Bows in the U.S. National Museum"; *Annual Report of the U.S. National Museum, 1884;* Washington, D.C., U.S. Government Printing Office

1892   "Ethnological Results of the Point Barrow Expedition"; *Ninth Annual Report of the U.S. Bureau of Ethnology, 1887-88;* Washington, D.C., U.S. Government Printing Office

Nelson, E.W.

1897   Letter to Walter Hoffman in Walter Hoffman, "Graphic Art of the Eskimos"; *Annual Report of the U.S. National Museum, 1895;* Washington, D.C., U.S. Government Printing Office

1899   "The Eskimo About Bering Strait"; *Eighteenth Annual Report of the U.S. Bureau of American Ethnology, 1896-97;* Washington, D.C., U.S. Government Printing office

Nordenskiöld, N.A.E.

1882   *The Voyage of the Vega around Asia and Europe* . . . ; New York, Macmillan

Oquilluk, William

1973   *People of Kauwerak: Legends of the Northern Eskimo;* Anchorage, Alaska Methodist University Press

Orth, Donald

1971   *Dictionary of Alaska Place Names;* Geological Survey Professional Paper 567; Washington, D.C., U.S. Government Printing Office

Parry, William Edward

1821   *Journal of a Voyage for the Discovery of a Northwest Passage* . . . *1819-20;* London, John Murray

1824   *Journal of a Second Voyage for the Discovery of a Northwest Passage* . . . *1821-22-23;* London, John Murray

Peard, George

1973   *To the Pacific and Arctic with Beechey: The Journal of Lieutenant George Peard of H.M.S. "Blossom" 1825-1828;* Barry Gough (ed.); Cambridge, Hakluyt Society

Petitot, E.F.S.J.

1876   *Monographie des Esquimaux Tchiglit du Mackenzie et de L'Anderson;* Paris, E. Leroux

1883   "Parallele des Coutumes et des Croyances de la famille Caraibo-Esquimaude avec celles des peoples Altaiques et Puniques." *Association Francaise pour l'Avancement des Sciences, Rouen 12^e session, 1883, seance du 23 août*

Pitt Rivers Museum

n.d.   Catalogue of Accessions; ms.

Rainey, Froelich

1947   "The Whale Hunters of Tigara"; *Anthropological Papers of the American Museum of Natural History*, vol. 41, part 2

n.d.   Field notes, 1940; ms.

Ray, Dorothy Jean

1964   "Nineteenth Century Settlement and Subsistence Patterns in Bering Strait"; *Arctic Anthropology*, vol. 2, no. 2

1966   "H.M.W. Edmonds' Report on the Eskimos of St. Michael and Vicinity"; Dorothy Jean Ray (ed.); *Anthropological Papers of the University of Alaska*, vol. 13, no. 2

1967   "Land Tenure and Polity of the Bering Strait Eskimo"; *Journal of the West*, vol. 4, no. 3

1969   "Graphic Arts of the Alaskan Eskimo"; *Native American Arts*, no. 2; Washington, D.C., U.S. Department of the Interior

1971   "Eskimo Place-Names in Bering Strait and Vicinity"; *Names*, vol. 19, no. 1

1975   "Early Maritime Trade with the Eskimo of Bering Strait and the Introduction of Firearms"; *Arctic Anthropology*, vol. 12, no. 1

n.d.*a*.   Personal communication

n.d.*b*.   *Arts of the North Alaskan Eskimos: Heritage and Innovation;* in press, University of Washington Press, Seattle

Ray, Patrick Henry

1885   *Report of the International Polar Expedition to Point Barrow, Alaska;* Washington, D.C., U.S. Government Printing Office

Richardson, John

1839   *The Zoology of Captain Beechey's Voyage;* London, H.G. Bohn

Sarychev, G. A.
1856   Atlas Severnoy Chasti Vostochnago Okean; St. Petersburg, Morskoy Tipografii

Ritchie, G.S.
1967   *The Admiralty Chart: British Naval Hydrography in the Nineteenth Century;* London, Hollis and Carter

Rosse, Irving C.
1883   "Medical and Anthropological Notes on Alaska"; *The Cruise of the Revenue Steamer Corwin in Alaska . . . 1881: Notes and Memoranda . . .* ; Washington, D.C., U.S. Government Printing Office

Rudenko, S.I.
1961   *The Ancient Culture of the Bering Sea and the Eskimo Problem;* Anthropology of the North: Translations from Russian Sources, no. 1; Toronto, Arctic Institute of North America and University of Toronto Press

Sauer, Martin
1802   *An Account of a Geographical and Astronomical Expedition to the Northern Parts of Russia . . .* ; London; T. Cadell, J. and W. Davis

Simpson, John
1854   "Observations on the Western Esquimaux and the Country They Inhabit, from notes taken during two years at Point Barrow"; *The Nautical Magazine and Naval Chronicle*, December

Simpson, Thomas
1843   *Narrative of Discoveries on the North Coast of America . . . 1836-39;* London, R. Bentley

Smyth, William
1831   "Narrative of the Proceedings of the barge of H.M.S. Blossom in quest of Captain Franklin, and to explore the Coast N.E. of Icy Cape"; in Frederick William Beechey, *Narrative of a Voyage to the Pacific and Beering's Strait . . . ;* London, Colburn and Bentley

n.d.*a.*   Journal of the voyage of H.M.S. *Blossom*, 1826; quoted in Richard Beechey, "Remarks on a Voyage of Discovery to the Pacific and Bhering's Straits . . ."; Public Record Office of Northern Ireland, Belfast

n.d.*b.*   Journal of the voyage of H.M.S. *Blossom*; quoted in James Wolfe, "Journal of a Voyage on Discovery in the Pacific and Beering's Straits on Board H.M.S. Blossom Capt. F.W. Beechey"; Beineke Rare Book and Manuscript Library, Yale University, New Haven

n.d.(*c*)   *Sketches of Natural History by Wm. Smyth Mate of H.M.S. Blossom;* ms. British Museum (Natural History)

Sonnenfeld, Joseph
1957   "Changes in Subsistence among the Barrow Eskimo"; Ph.D. dissertation, Faculty of Philosophy, The Johns Hopkins University, Baltimore

Spencer, Robert
1959   *The North Alaskan Eskimo: A Study in Ecology and Society;* Smithsonian Institution, Bureau of American Ethnology, Bulletin 171; Washington D.C., U.S. Government Printing Office

Stefansson, Vilhjalmur
1909   "Northern Alaska in Winter"; *Bulletin of the American Geographical Society*, vol. 41, no. 10
1914   "The Stefansson-Anderson Arctic Expedition of the American Museum: Preliminary Ethnological Report"; *Anthropological Papers of the American Museum of Natural History*, vol. 14, part 1

Stuart-Stubbs, Basil
1972   "Sir Edward Belcher" *Dictionary of Canadian Biography;* Marc La Terreur (ed.); vol. 10; Toronto, University of Toronto Press

Taylor, J. Garth
1974   *Netsilik Eskimo Material Culture;* Oslo, Universitetforlaget

Thalbitzer, William
1914   "Ethnographical Collections from East Greenland"; *Meddelelser om Grønland*, vol. 39, pt. 7

Thornton, Harrison R.
1931   *Among the Eskimos of Wales, Alaska;* Baltimore, The Johns Hopkins Press

Tikhmenev, P.
1939-40   *The Historical Review of Formation of the Russian American Company* ... ; Dimitri Krenov (trans.), ms. Microfilm, Library of Congress, Washington, D.C.

VanStone, James W.
1973   "V.S. Khromchenko's Coastal Explorations in Southwestern Alaska, 1822"; *Fieldiana: Anthropology*, vol. 64, November 23
n.d.   "A.F. Kashevarov's Coastal Explorations in North West Alaska, 1838"; typescript

Van Valin, William
n.d.   Photographs of ethnographic specimens; Van Valin Collection, Archives, Library of the University of Alaska, Fairbanks

Whymper, Frederick
1869   *Travel and Adventure in the Territory of Alaska* ... ; London, John Murray

Woldt, A.
1884   *Captain Jacobsen's Reise an der Nordwestküste Amerikas 1881-1883* ... ; Leipzig, Max Spohr

Wolfe, James
n.d.   "Journal of a Voyage on Discovery in the Pacific and Beering's Straits on board H.M.S. Blossom Capt. F.W. Beechey"; Beinecke Rare Book and Manuscript Library, Yale University, New Haven
n.d.*a.*   Journal kept on board H.M.S. *Blossom*; quoted in Richard Beechey, "Remarks on a Voyage of Discovery to the Pacific and Behring's Straits ... ; Public Record Office of Northern Ireland, Belfast

Wrangell, Ferdinand von
1840   *Narrative of an Expedition to the Polar Sea in the years 1820, 1821, 1822, & 1823;* London, James Madden

Yefimov, A.V.
1964   *Atlas of Geographical Discoveries in Siberia and Northwestern America: XVII-XVIII Centuries;* Moscow, Nauka

Zagoskin, L.A.
1967   *Lieutenant Zagoskin's Travels in Russian America, 1842-1844* ... ; Anthropology of the North: Translations from Russian Sources, no. 7; Toronto, Arctic Institute of North America and University of Toronto Press